C000230317

'Kay Plunkett-Hogge's cooking – and knowledge – of Thai cuisine is next to none. I dream about her food. Thank God she's written this book.' *Diana Henry*

'This book makes me hungry. Truly a beautiful, personal, delicious and easy-to-use guide to Thai cuisine full of stories and tips that make the food jump off the page and onto the plate.' *Ian Kittichai*

'Wise, witty, and wonderfully written, *Baan* sits alongside David Thompson's *Thai Food* and Andy Ricker's *Pok Pok* as one of the great English language works on regional Thai cookery.' *Tom Parker-Bowles*

'Kay's true home is Thailand. Rarely have I met some with such a love of a country, its people and their food. This book, so aptly named *Baan*, is the result of her journey through the Kingdom and many kitchens. It is home cooking, the true source of the best of Thai food. Kay recounts the charm, delicious fun and spirit of Thai kitchens in this book. I am captivated.' *David Thompson*

บ้าน
Baan

**Recipes and stories
from my Thai home**

Kay Plunkett-Hogge

PAVILION

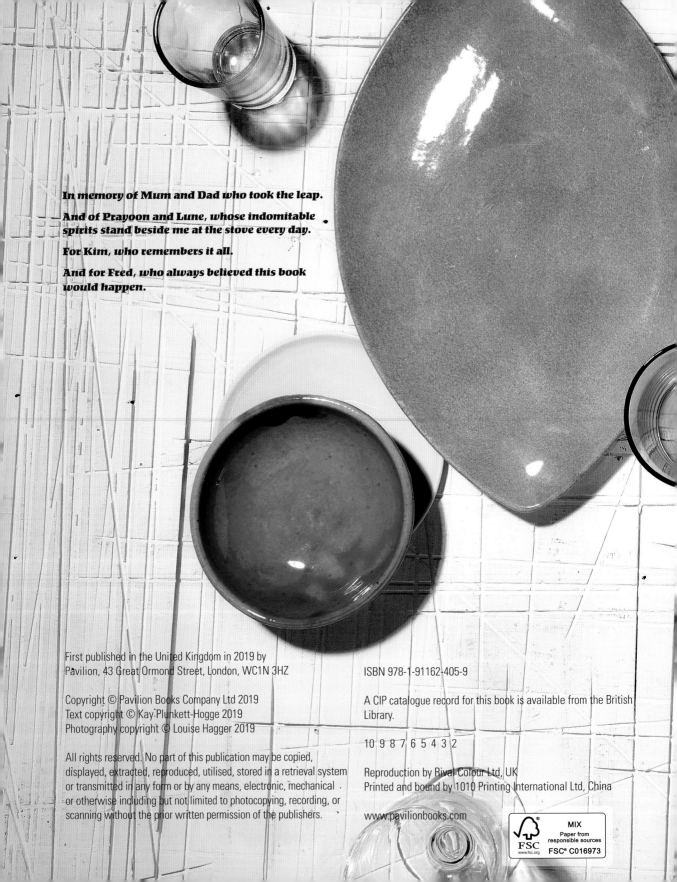

In memory of Mum and Dad who took the leap.

And of Prayoon and Lune, whose indomitable spirits stand beside me at the stove every day.

For Kim, who remembers it all.

And for Fred, who always believed this book would happen.

First published in the United Kingdom in 2019 by Pavilion, 43 Great Ormond Street, London, WC1N 3HZ

Copyright © Pavilion Books Company Ltd 2019
Text copyright © Kay Plunkett-Hogge 2019
Photography copyright © Louise Hagger 2019

All rights reserved. No part of this publication may be copied, displayed, extracted, reproduced, utilised, stored in a retrieval system or transmitted in any form or by any means, electronic, mechanical or otherwise including but not limited to photocopying, recording, or scanning without the prior written permission of the publishers.

ISBN 978-1-91162-405-9

A CIP catalogue record for this book is available from the British Library.

10 9 8 7 6 5 4 3 2

Reproduction by Rival Colour Ltd, UK
Printed and bound by 1010 Printing International Ltd, China

www.pavilionbooks.com

FSC
www.fsc.org

MIX
Paper from responsible sources
FSC® C016973

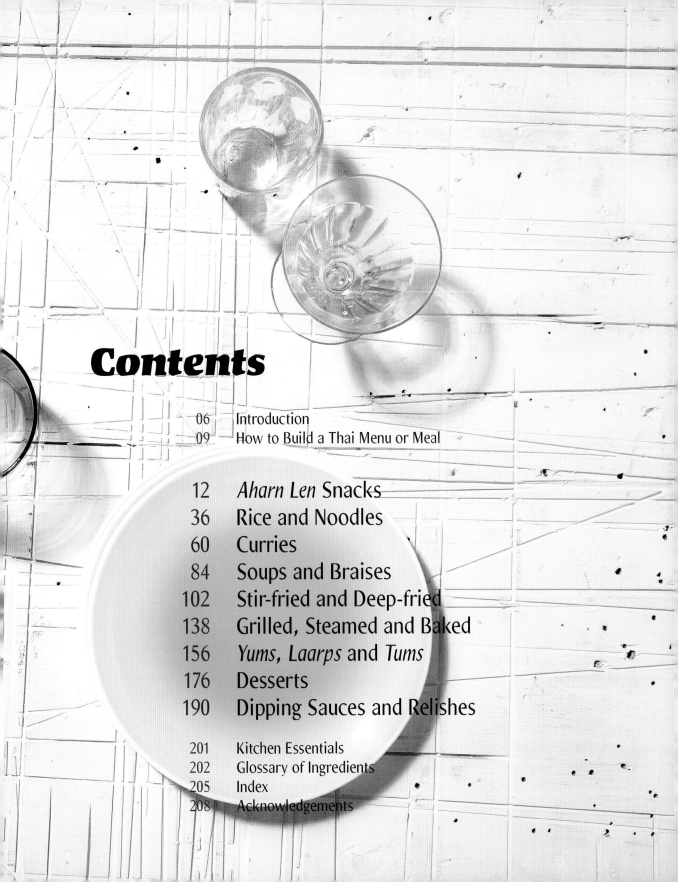

Contents

The word *baan* means a house or a home. It can also mean a village.

But it goes deeper than that: it's a word that stems from the various dialects of the Tai language family. *Baan* means the hearth, the home, the community, the place where you come from.

It speaks to how we sustain each other. It speaks to the ties that bind us together. It speaks to the heart.

Which, to me, is where food comes from.

This is a book about home cooking. It also happens to be about Thai food. For, while I have written before about Spanish food, Italian food and so on, it is Thai food that I cook most often.

I was born and raised in Bangkok. I spoke Thai before I spoke English (which freaked out my Irish grandmother when I was brought to London for the first time aged three). I have spent more than half my life in Thailand, as a child, as a young professional in the film business, and latterly as a food writer and journalist.

And I have been very privileged that my work has allowed me to travel the length and breadth of the country. More so, that the language has opened more doors for me there, both literally and figuratively, than the average white-faced girl has ever had the chance to walk through.

As a result, I have been able to collect recipes from wherever I've been: from tribal Tai Yai and Akha people in the mountains of the Golden Triangle; from elephant *kwans* in the forests of Lampang Province; from fishermen in coastal Ranong; from stall holders, chefs, shop keepers, air stewards, taxi drivers, chambermaids, horsemen, *hi-so* women; from little old ladies in markets; and from people who have kindly called me *na farang hua jai Thai* — the foreign-faced girl with the heart of a Thai.

This book is the result of all those conversations. And it's the result of many happy hours spent in the kitchen with Prayoon, our family cook, when I was a chubby, greedy little girl, helping to stoke the charcoal braziers, to pound chillies and garlic, or to chop herbs. That she indulged me, instead of shooing me out the door for being underfoot, has left me with a lasting love of Thai cooking.

SEP · 69

Most importantly, every recipe has been tested in my London kitchen on a now 15-year-old four-gas-hob Smeg with its single electric oven (apart from some of the grill recipes, which I cooked on the barbecue). But whatever your kitchen set-up, the single most important piece of advice I could give you is to taste, taste, taste everything and adjust as you like.

Aiming high, I hope it achieves Julia Child's goal for a book, of being 'for those who love to cook', with recipes that are 'as detailed as they should be so that the reader knows exactly what is involved and how to go about it.'

That Julia knew a thing or two.

More importantly, instead of setting out to 'simplify' Thai cooking, I aim to demystify it a little, providing clear recipes and revealing the short-cuts, kitchen hacks and ingredient substitutions that make it achievable in an ordinary Western kitchen. Some of the recipes will be familiar, some unusual, and some so regional they capture a distinct sliver of Thailand and its unique character. And all of them are well within the capabilities of the competent and curious cook.

Most important of all, I have endeavoured to write a book to be *used*. My highest hope is for it to sit on your shelf, tattered and stained, with pages dog-eared at the corners and the spine half falling off.

I hope to guide you – the cook, the reader – deeper into Thai cooking, a world of fragrant curry pastes, fiery soups, and dishes of profound and gracious subtlety, and on to a culinary adventure in the comfort of your very own kitchen.

And, of course, *chan wang wa khun cha sanuk kub nung sueh* – I hope you have fun with it.

How to Build a Thai Menu or Meal

I sometimes have a little difficulty with serving suggestions. I mean, how can I possibly know how much you like to eat? When it comes to Thai food, it's harder still because context is everything. When cooking for two, for example, I might cook one of the stir-fries and a mug of rice. And perhaps a deep-fried egg each, depending on the dish. For a Sunday curry lunch, I'd make one batch of curry and a vegetable dish (and rice), again for two, knowing I'll have curry left over.

As a general rule of thumb, if I'm cooking for just the two of us, I'll do two or three things, depending on how greedy we're feeling. For four, I'll do three of four dishes; for six, six or seven dishes, and so on – but now we're getting to the stage when I need Fred's help, or I'll never get to sit down and enjoy my friends' company. In each case, the rice is an extra and essential thing to do.

Here are some examples, based on how I cook Thai for my family. Bear in mind that they're just suggestions. Mix and match your menu to suit your tastes and curiosities.

One plate dishes for two: *Khao Pad Goong* (Page 45) with a *kai dao* (Page 133) each; *Pad Krapow* (Page 118), also with a *kai dao* each and served with rice; *Pad Thai* (Page 50); *Pad Kee Mao* (Page 52). Each of these recipes serves two in this context — if you want to make them for four, make them in two batches. If you double the ingredients in one wok, it won't work.

Sunday Lunch or dinner for two: *Gaeng Pet* (Page 66) (there will be leftovers), *Pad Pak Ruan Mit* (Page 112), *Kai Jeow* (Page 134) and rice.

Lunch or dinner for four: *Gaeng Keow Wan* (Page 63), *Pad Pak Boong Fai Daeng* (Page 113), a *laarp* and/or a *yum* of your choice — in the latter case it depends on what looks good in the shops — rice, and *Som Loey Kaew* (Page 178) for dessert.

Dinner for six to eight: this is where I'd pull out some of the big guns *Gaeng Massaman* (Page 70) with roti (Page 71), *Pad Pak Khana Pla Kem* (Page 125), *Kai Toon* (Page 147) or *Gaeng Cheud Mara* (Page 88) for something neutral, *Neua Tom Kem* (Page 97), *Yum Hua Plee* (Page 159), Khun Nai's squid (Page 137) and rice. I'd also make a couple of Aharn Len dishes to stave off the guests' hunger pangs while I finish cooking, as well as, perhaps, a nam prik or two with crudities. And definitely dessert, probably something like the Mango, Lime and Basil Sorbet (Page 186) or the *Nam Kang Gno* (Page 189), because they're refreshing and cleansing. Alternatively, I will do a big batch of *Kow Soi* (Page 56) with all the bits that go with it. It's much more casual, and great fun. In this case, I'd also make *Nam Prik Num* (Page 196) and *Nam Prik Ong* (Page 198), served with crudities and *Kap Moo* (Page 128), the last of which I often buy in, and perhaps a *laarp* (Pages 166–8), and fresh fruit to finish.

My dinner table's in the kitchen, so I'm not sequestered away from my friends, and I can get them to muck in if I need to. Either way, things are ready when they're ready. As long as you've done all your prep, ideally made the curry the day before, have some good tunes on the iPod and the wine flowing, all will be well.

Aharn Len

Snacks

Goong Cha Nam Pla

Thai-style Prawn Sashimi
with Fish Sauce

Thais love to snack. It doesn't matter whether it's a mid-morning wrapper of deep-fried banana, or an afternoon stick of grilled (broiled) pork, or a hastily grabbed bag of green mango with chilli salt to tide one over until dinner, snacks are available all day and, in the cities at least, all night.

Don't be put off by the fact that these prawns (shrimp) are served raw. The *nam pla*, lime and chillies have an almost ceviche-like curing effect upon them, which is utterly delicious. Do make sure you get the freshest prawns you can. Serve with a frosty glass of Thai beer.

Serves 4 (approx. 2 each)

300 g/10½ oz raw king prawns (jumbo shrimp), peeled, de-veined and butterflied with tail on, chilled

6 Thai bird's eye chillies, finely chopped

5 garlic cloves, peeled and finely chopped

1 coriander (cilantro) root (see page 203), finely chopped

1 tsp palm sugar

1 tbsp *nam pla* (fish sauce)

juice of 1 lime

lettuce leaves or shredded cabbage, to serve

a handful of mint leaves, to serve

First, prepare and chill the prawns, as directed.

In a small bowl, thoroughly mix the chillies, garlic and coriander root together. Add the palm sugar, *nam pla* and lime juice and mix well until the sugar has dissolved. Taste: you want a nice balance of hot, salty and sour, with the sour a little more pronounced.

Arrange the chilled prawns on top of the lettuce or cabbage. Pour or spoon the dressing over them, top with the mint leaves and serve straight away.

Kanom Jeep

Thai Steamed Dumplings

These are, essentially, Thai-style dim sum. I suspect they're descended from Chinese *shao mai* dumplings, which themselves originated in Mongolia. It's hardly surprising that something so delicious should have travelled so far, evolving on the way to produce variations across southeast Asia. They're also very simple to make, which is a bonus.

Makes 18–24

1 coriander (cilantro) root (see page 203)

1 tsp white peppercorns

1 garlic clove, peeled

a pinch of salt

5-mm/¼-inch piece of fresh ginger, peeled

250 g/9 oz minced (ground) pork

100 g/3½ oz raw prawns (shrimp),
   finely chopped

3–4 water chestnuts, finely chopped

1 tbsp *nam pla* (fish sauce)

a pinch of sugar

18–24 won ton wrappers

for the garlic oil

2 tbsp vegetable oil

3 garlic cloves, finely chopped

for the dipping sauce

2 tbsp light soy sauce

2 tbsp dark soy sauce

2 tbsp white vinegar or rice vinegar

1 tbsp sugar

a little chopped fresh coriander (cilantro)

½ large red chilli, deseeded and sliced

In a pestle and mortar, pound together the coriander root, peppercorns, garlic, salt and ginger until you have a paste.

In a large bowl, mix the paste together with the pork, prawns, water chestnuts, *nam pla* and sugar. Set aside.

To make the garlic oil, heat the oil in a wok and fry the garlic just until golden brown. Remove from the heat, pour the garlic and oil into a bowl and set aside.

To make the dipping sauce, add the light and dark soy sauce, vinegar and sugar to a small bowl and stir until combined and the sugar has dissolved. Stir in the chopped coriander and the red chilli slices. Set aside.

To make the dumplings, touch your thumb and forefinger together to form an 'O'-shaped hole. Take one won ton wrapper at a time and drape it over the hole. Put a nugget of filling in the middle of the sheet, pushing down slightly and then crimp the edges as you pass the dumpling through the hole. Carry on until you have filled all the sheets or used up all the fillling.

Place the *kanoms* in a steamer over boiling water, and steam until done – about 10 minutes.

Serve immediately, with the garlic oil drizzled over the top and the dipping sauce on the side.

Prayoon's Tod Mun Pla

Prayoon's Fish Cakes

I have yet to find a better recipe for Thai fish cakes than this version, taught to me by our cook Prayoon when I was 12.

Like she did, I always use a good-quality bought red curry paste for this. Making it fresh just for fishcakes seems like a faff. But if you want to, the recipe is on page 66.

The secret to a proper Thai fishcake is its texture. It has to be spongy, almost rubbery, far removed from the flaky Western-style things one often finds in pubs.

Makes 16–18, depending on size

250 g/9 oz skinless white fish fillets
2 heaped tbsp red curry paste
  (store-bought or see page 66)
1 egg
1 tbsp green beans, sliced
1 tbsp kaffir lime leaves, finely sliced
  (see tip)
1 tsp sugar
a pinch of salt
1–2 tbsp *nam pla* (fish sauce), to taste
oil, for deep-frying

Put the fish, curry paste and egg into a food processor and blitz into a homogenised paste. Remove to a clean bowl, then stir in the beans and the lime leaves, then add the sugar, a pinch of salt and 1 tbsp of *nam pla*.

Heat a little oil in a wok, and fry off a piece of the mixture to check the seasoning. Different curry pastes have different balances of flavour. Add more *nam pla* or sugar if you need to.

Now slap the mixture around the bowl a bit to aerate it – this is how you achieve the puffy, springy texture of a classic Thai fish cake. Wet your hands slightly, and form the fish paste into flattish patties. You choose the size – you can have them as big as a plate or bite-sized. I prefer to use this quantity of the mixture to make 16–18 smaller ones, because I like to serve them with drinks.

Heat the oil in a wok until it's hot – if you're using a deep-fryer, set it to 180°C/350°F. Fry the fish cakes in batches until puffy and brown. Transfer them to paper towels as you go, then serve straight away with *Ajad* (Quick Pickled Cucumber, page 193), as pictured, on the side.

~ The best way to slice a lime leaf is to roll it up lengthways, like a tight cigar, and then cut it into thin strips. If you attempt to attack it flat on your chopping board, it will irritate the hell out of you. ~

~ In Hua Hin, one of my favourite Thai seaside towns, the locals make a slightly different version of this recipe. Replace half the fish with prawns (shrimp), and add 1–2 tbsp of toasted, grated coconut to the mix. Traditionally this is then moulded on to sticks of sugarcane before grilling (broiling), but you can just fry them off as above. ~

Tod Mun Fukthong Khun Tavee

Khun Tavee's Pumpkin Fritters

The Karen hill tribes have been migrating into northern Thailand since the seventeenth century, but originally they came from the mountains of south-eastern Myanmar, with which Thailand shares a border. Like many of the northern hill tribes, theirs is not a happy story, and far too complicated and political for a cookery book. Suffice to say that many have fled oppression in Myanmar to live as refugees in Thailand and elsewhere.

Their cooking is distinct from Thai, as exemplified by this dish, which I got from Khun Tavee, the mother of my friend Ae, who works as a tour guide in Chiang Mai.

Like the Akha, another of the northern hill tribes, the Karen do not use fish sauce. And, given their traditional reliance on rotational agriculture, theirs is a very vegetable-heavy cuisine. Which might explain why these fritters just happen to be vegan.

Khun Tavee tells me that you can also make this with the same amount of shredded banana flowers. I have not tried it, primarily because when I find a banana flower of sufficient quality, I tend to make the *Yum Hua Plee* (Banana Blossom Salad, page 159)!

Makes 16–18

4 green Thai bird's eye chillies, sliced

3 garlic cloves, peeled and finely chopped

a good pinch of salt

a good pinch of sugar

300 g/10½ oz grated or shredded pumpkin (about 600 g/1 lb 5 oz unpeeled)

2 tbsp glutinous (sticky) rice flour

6 tbsp rice flour

vegetable oil, for deep-frying

In a pestle and mortar, lightly crush together the chillies, garlic, salt and sugar. Scrape into a bowl with the grated pumpkin and stir gently to combine. Add the glutinous (sticky) rice flour and the rice flour, then stir in enough water to make a soft, dropping consistency.

Heat the oil in a wok until it's hot – if you're using a deep-fryer, set it to 180°C/350°F. Form the mixture into loose patties and fry until crisp and golden. Remove to drain on paper towels.

Serve with *Ajad* (Quick Pickled Cucumber, page 193) – noting that, for this dish, it's made slightly differently, as you will see.

Oysters with Mee's 'Mignonette'

Mee's Sauce for Oysters

My friend Mee (Somjai Kliangklom) made this when we were going for a picnic on a tiny island off Ranong in southern Thailand. Once there, he opened oysters with a machete, added a dab off his special 'mignonette' and topped it with a garnish that included fronds of *kratin*, or horse tamarind, which he'd just picked moments before.

The *kratin* blew my mind. It enhances the oyster's creaminess, which in turn offsets the fire of the chillies, to create a harmony of flavour I had never before experienced. You can find *kratin* at most good Asian supermarkets – but if you can't, go without.

Makes 12

6 Thai shallots, or 3 regular shallots, finely sliced

12 fresh oysters, shucked

oil, for deep-frying

for the 'mignonette'

6–8 Thai bird's eye chillies

3 large garlic cloves, peeled

2 tbsp caster (superfine) sugar

juice of 2 limes, plus more to taste

1 tsp *nam pla* (fish sauce), plus more to taste

for the additional garnishes

a few garlic cloves, finely sliced

2 limes, cut into small segments, with the membrane removed

12 fronds of *kratin* (horse tamarind) (optional)

2–3 spring onions (scallions), very finely sliced

To make the 'mignonette', pound the chillies and the garlic in a pestle and mortar until smooth. Add the sugar and pound again. Add the lime juice and *nam pla*, and taste, adding more of the lime juice and nam pla if necessary. Set aside.

Heat the oil in a wok or frying pan (skillet) and, when it's hot, deep-fry the sliced shallots, stirring them all the time, until they are golden and crispy. Remove to drain on paper towels.

Serve the oysters with a drizzle of the 'mignonette', garnished with a little bit of everything else.

Peek Gai

Chicken Wings

These are sticky and delicious, and perfect with a cold beer. I've based their seasoning on some fried chicken knuckles I once had at the Saxophone Jazz and Blues Pub near the Victory Monument. Serve with either *Nam Jim Jaew* (Roasted Chilli Dipping Sauce) (Page 194) or sweet chilli sauce.

Serves 4

800 g/1 lb 12 oz chicken wings, jointed
   (approx. 10–12)

for the marinade
4 tbsp light soy sauce
2 tbsp sweet soy sauce
1 tbsp oyster sauce
1 tbsp *Laarp Kua* spice mix
   (Northern-Style *Laarp*, page 167)
4 tbsp *nam pla* (fish sauce)
2 tbsp tamarind paste (purée)
1 tbsp palm sugar

In a large bowl, thoroughly combine all the marinade ingredients. Stir the chicken wings through the marinade, cover and marinate in the fridge for at least 1 hour.

Preheat the grill (broiler) to medium.

Grill (broil) the wings for 15–20 minutes, turning from time to time, and basting with any excess marinade if you like, until cooked through and the juices run clear.

Laarp Grop Song

Two Types of Crispy Pork
Laarp Balls

Crispy on the outside, soft and fragrant in the middle, these meatballs are my idea of snack heaven, and a million miles away from soggy vol au vents or cheesy puffs. They were originally designed to use up leftover *laarp* which, in my experience, never happens. So I came up with this.

Makes approx. 18

Isaan-style Laarp

250 g/9 oz minced (ground) pork
1 heaped tbsp chopped fresh mint, leaves only
2 tsp toasted rice powder (see tip on page 166)
1 tbsp chopped Thai or regular shallots
1 tbsp lime juice
1 tbsp *nam pla* (fish sauce)
1 tsp roasted chilli powder (available in Asian supermarkets)
1 tbsp rice flour, for lightly coating
vegetable oil, for deep-frying

to serve
lettuce leaves
lime wedges

In a large bowl, mix together all the ingredients, except the flour and oil, with your hands, making sure everything is well incorporated.

Heat a little oil in a small frying pan (skillet) and fry off a small piece of the mixture to taste. It should taste sharp, nutty, spicy and salty. Adjust the seasoning as necessary. Shape the mixture into about 18 evenly sized meatballs, a bit smaller in size than a ping pong ball. Roll the balls in the rice flour, tapping off any excess.

Heat the oil for deep-frying in a small wok until hot, then deep-fry the meatballs in batches until deep golden, crisp and cooked through. Drain on paper towels, then serve with lettuce leaves, lime wedges and *Nam Jim Jaew* (Roasted Chilli Dipping Sauce, page 194) on the side, if you like.

Northern-style Laarp Kua

250 g/9 oz minced (ground) pork
1 tbsp *Laarp Kua* spice mix
   (Northern-Style *Laarp*, page 167)
2 kaffir lime leaves, finely sliced
1 tbsp chopped fresh mint, leaves only
1 tbsp chopped fresh coriander (cilantro)
1 spring onion (scallion), finely chopped
1 tbsp deep-fried garlic (page 204)
1 tbsp *nam pla* (fish sauce)
1 tbsp rice flour, for lightly coating
vegetable oil, for frying

to serve
lettuce leaves
lime wedges

In a large bowl, mix together all the ingredients, except the flour and oil, with your hands, making sure everything is well incorporated.

Heat a little oil in a small frying pan (skillet) and fry off a small piece of the mixture to taste. It should taste aromatic, spicy and salty. Adjust the seasoning as necessary.

Shape, cook and serve following the method opposite for Isaan-style *Laarp*.

Miang Khum

'Little Bites'

This dish is a DIY delight – tasty morsels, served separately for you to wrap up on a leaf, dress with the sauce and devour. Often you'll find its component parts sold in small packages from street vendors, ready to assemble. Each one offers a rainbow of flavour.

The dish's roots lie in the north. The star ingredient is the leaves: *bai chaploo*, or wild pepper leaves, which can be found in good Asian supermarkets. Not to be confused with betel leaves, though they look similar; betel has a more pronounced and tongue-numbing flavour. These guys are lightly peppery and more subtle, and are so associated with this dish that some people call them simply *bai miang*. If you can't find them, make do with spinach leaves.

As for the fillings, you can replace the dried shrimp with some flaked, hot-smoked mackerel, or serve both, and you can add a few small segments of pomelo or grapefruit to the mix too.

Serves 6–8

32 wild pepper leaves (*bai chaploo*),
  or spinach leaves

for the sauce

2 tsp *kapi* (shrimp paste)

1 banana leaf (optional)

2.5-cm/1-inch piece of fresh ginger,
  peeled and finely chopped

2.5-cm/1-inch piece of galangal, peeled
  and finely chopped

1 stick lemongrass, finely chopped

2 Thai shallots or 1 regular shallot, peeled
  and finely chopped

100–125 ml/3½–4 fl oz/⅓–½ cup *nam pla*
  (fish sauce)

1–2 tsp tamarind paste (purée)

125 g/4½ oz palm sugar

1 tbsp peanuts, toasted, lightly crushed

1 tbsp shredded, unsweetened coconut,
  toasted until brown

for the fillings

4 tbsp dried prawns (shrimp), fried

4 Thai shallots or 2 regular shallots,
  peeled and finely chopped

4 tbsp shredded, unsweetened coconut,
  toasted until golden

4 tbsp sliced Thai bird's eye chillies

4 tbsp unsalted peanuts, toasted

2 limes, sliced, chopped into segments

2.5-cm/1-inch piece of fresh ginger,
  peeled and finely chopped

To make the sauce, wrap the *kapi* in the banana leaf or aluminium foil. Toast in a dry frying pan (skillet) until fragrant – the banana leaf will char. Set aside.

Toast the ginger, galangal, lemongrass and shallots in the same dry pan until they're just turning colour. Transfer to a pestle and mortar and pound into a fine paste.

Heat a saucepan over a gentle heat and add the *kapi*, ginger paste, *nam pla*, tamarind paste and palm sugar. Stir until you have a sticky sauce. If it seems thick, add a dash of water – you want it to be like runny honey. Stir in the peanuts and the coconut. Transfer to a bowl and cool.

To serve, place the leaves on a platter with the filling ingredients and divide the sauce among a few small bowls. Take a leaf and add a selection of the filling ingredients. Dress with the sauce, wrap the leaf around its contents and eat in one bite.

Ma Hor
'Galloping Horses'

This dish was a staple of many a Plunkett cocktail party when I was small – the most delicious morsels of sweet, salty, almost candied pork on sharp wedges of pineapple and orange.

The name translates literally as 'galloping horses'. Our cook Prayoon used to say that it was because of the recipe's Chinese influence, and that the Chinese traders who brought their horse caravans down through northern Thailand were known as '*Jeen Hor*', or 'the Galloping Chinese'. Another friend said it was because the pork was riding the fruit and the dish was quick to make. I rather like both stories. You choose.

If they're in season, try to use blood oranges for this. They taste delicious and look like jewels.

Makes about 36

3 coriander (cilantro) roots (see page 203), finely chopped

3 garlic cloves, peeled

1 tsp white peppercorns

2 tbsp vegetable oil

3 Thai shallots or 1 regular shallot, peeled and finely sliced (optional)

250 g/9 oz minced (ground) pork, or mixture of minced (ground) pork and minced (ground) prawns

2 tbsp *nam pla* (fish sauce)

4 tbsp palm sugar

1 tbsp roasted peanuts, smashed

to serve

1 pineapple, trimmed, cored, sliced and cut into bite-sized pieces

2–4 oranges, peeled and sliced fairly thickly

1 long red chilli, deseeded and finely sliced

a handful of fresh coriander (cilantro) leaves

Using a pestle and mortar, pound the coriander root, garlic and peppercorns together to form a paste.

In a wok or a frying pan (skillet), heat the oil and cook the paste for a couple of minutes until fragrant. Add the shallots, if using, and stir them into the paste for 30 seconds or so to combine. Add the pork, or pork and prawns, and stir it into the paste until well incorporated. Add the *nam pla* and palm sugar, stirring and frying until the meat is cooked. You're looking to achieve a texture akin to a pork jam. If you think it needs more palm sugar, add it; more *nam pla*, the same. You want a salty, sweet, sticky mass.

Add the peanuts, and continue to cook until it becomes quite thick, like fudge. Remove from the heat, and let the mixture cool completely. You can do all this well ahead of time, even the day before you want to serve it, just keep it refrigerated once cooled. You can also keep the fruit slices refrigerated for ease.

Just before serving, complete the dish. Roll the pork mixture into balls of appropriate size to fit on the pineapple and orange pieces. Then garnish with a sliver of chilli and a coriander leaf. Serve at once.

Sai Oua

Spiced Northern Thai Sausage

There are few things that please my guests more than a large, warm coil of *Sai Oua* sausage on a plate on the living room table, a sharp knife lying next to it, ready for everyone to slice into and demolish while they sip on a cold Tom Collins. Or a Martini.

If you can't or don't want to make the actual sausage, feel free to divide the pork mixture into patties and cook like little burgers. If you do, your butcher will be able to sell you the sausage casings.

Makes 1 large coiled sausage, or 2 regular ones

4 coriander (cilantro) roots
   (see page 203), chopped

4 Thai shallots or 2 regular shallots,
   peeled and chopped

4-cm/1½-inch piece of galangal, peeled
   and finely chopped

2 sticks lemongrass, bashed
   and chopped

2 garlic cloves, peeled and chopped

2-cm/¾-inch piece of fresh turmeric,
   chopped

1 large red chilli, deseeded
   and chopped

2 tbsp good-quality red curry paste

4 tbsp cooked rice

1½ tbsp *nam pla* (fish sauce)

500 g/1 lb 2 oz minced (ground) pork,
   with a good bit of fat in it

a big pinch of salt

8–12 kaffir lime leaves, very finely sliced

natural sausage casings

vegetable oil, for deep-frying (optional)

to serve
chopped lettuces
chopped cabbage
mint leaves
fresh coriander (cilantro) leaves

Using a pestle and mortar, pound the coriander roots, shallots, galangal, lemongrass, garlic, turmeric and fresh chilli to a rough paste. Stir through the red curry paste, cooked rice and *nam pla*.

In a large bowl, combine the pork with the spice paste and the salt, and mix thoroughly. Add the sliced lime leaves and stir through.

At this point, I suggest frying off a small piece of the mixture so you can taste it and adjust the seasoning, if necessary. You want it fragrant, herbal, and a little spicy.

Now, using a sausage machine or a funnel, put the sausagemeat into the casings, making sure you smooth out any air bubbles. Twist the sausage at the halfway point if you want two sausages, or form it into a larger coil like a Cumberland sausage. Tie the skin at the end into a knot.

When you're ready to cook, poke a few holes in the sausage with a bamboo stick, and then either grill over a charcoal fire – medium coals – for about 25–30 minutes until done (this is my preferred method, as it imparts a smoky flavour) *or* deep-fry in a wok with vegetable oil heated to about 160°C/320°F (a medium heat… if you go too hot, the sausage will burst).

Serve with a selection of chopped lettuces, cabbage, mint and coriander (cilantro).

~ *If your sausage does burst, don't fret, just style it out. It will still taste delicious.* ~

Naem Sot

Faux Cured Isaan Sausage

Naem, or *jin som*, is a sausage from northern and northeastern Thailand, which is cured or fermented with rice over the course of several days. It has a gloriously funky, sour taste, and I can't get enough of it. However, fermenting meat carries certain risks that I have never been entirely comfortable with when I'm cooking at home. And the ones available commercially here in the UK are not the best I've ever had (see tip below). So I was thrilled to find this recipe for a cheat's version, in revered teacher Srisamorn Kongpun's book *Bite-Sized Thai Food*, which I have adapted. Here, you cook the pork and mix in the traditional condiments. It tastes almost exactly like the real thing. So, when the craving hits, it can be dealt with lickety-split.

Makes 12–15

250 g/9 oz minced (ground) pork

juice of 4 limes

1 tsp salt

100 g/3½ oz boiled pork skin, finely sliced (optional)

3 garlic cloves, chopped

3 Thai shallots or 1 regular shallot, finely sliced

3 fresh Thai bird's eye chillies, finely sliced

2.5-cm/1-inch piece of fresh ginger, slivered

to serve

baby gem lettuce leaves

2 tbsp roasted unsalted peanuts

10 dried bird's eye (bird) chillies, deep-fried (optional)

fresh Thai bird's eye chillies

In a large bowl, thoroughly mix together the pork, lime juice and salt. Leave for 3–4 minutes, then squeeze out the resulting juice with your hands into a frying pan (skillet). Place it over a low heat, add the pork and gently cook, breaking the mince apart until it's done. Transfer to another large bowl and set aside to cool.

When the pork is cool enough to handle, add the pork skin, if using, followed by the garlic, two-thirds of the shallots, the fresh chilli and the ginger. Toss the mixture lightly together. Taste and adjust the seasoning — you want a top note of sour, then salt, and then the aromatics.

Serve it spooned into baby gem lettuce leaves and top with the peanuts, the remaining shallots, and the deep-fried chillies, if wished. Dot with fresh chillies, if you're feeling feisty, or serve them on the side for those that want them.

~ If you DO happen to buy some store-bought naem, try slicing it, wrapping the slices in streaky bacon and deep-frying them. Holy fermented pigs! It is so darn tasty. I picked this tip up from the award-winning chef at the Siri Sathorn, a serviced apartment block where I frequently stay in Bangkok. ~

Moo Muan Sukhothai

Deep-fried Pork Meatballs with White Pepper

The ancient Thai capital of Sukhothai is truly spectacular. Its thirteenth-century ruins are a UNESCO site visited by millions of tourists every year. So, I've always found it surprising that, these days, I can no longer find a decent restaurant there. That said, Pee Noi, the now-retired cook at the Tharaburi Resort, just outside the Historical Park, has in the past shown me proper regional Sukhothai food when the hotel has not been too busy.

This delicious meatball recipe is based on one of hers, and is best served with Sriracha sauce and an ice-cold beer.

Makes 18–24

1 tsp white peppercorns
2 garlic cloves, peeled
2 coriander (cilantro) roots
  (see page)
a pinch of salt
250 g/9 oz minced (ground) pork
1 tbsp *nam pla* (fish sauce)
a couple of dashes of light soy sauce
a good pinch of sugar
1 tbsp rice flour
vegetable oil, for deep-frying

In a pestle and mortar, pound together the peppercorns, coriander roots, garlic and salt until you have a paste.

In a large bowl, mix the paste into the pork with your hands – really squish it about to get it evenly distributed. Add the *nam pla*, soy and sugar and mix it in well. Form the pork into 2-cm/¾-inch balls, and roll them in the rice flour.

Heat the oil in a wok over a medium heat. When it is hot enough, fry the pork balls in small batches for about 1½–2 minutes each, or until deep brown on the outside and cooked through within. Transfer them to drain on paper towels as you go.

Serve hot with Sriracha sauce.

Neua Dat Deow

'Sun-Dried' Beef

Unless you live somewhere around the 15th Parallel, this is rather difficult to make at home because, done properly, you need to dry your beef in the sun. Even in sunny Los Angeles (34°N), I haven't made it work. But *neua* or *moo dat deow* is so delicious, we need to find a work-around, and this is it.

Serves 2–4

3 tbsp *nam pla* (fish sauce)

1 tbsp Mekong or Sangsom whisky (optional)

1 tbsp soy sauce

1 tsp palm sugar

½ tsp white peppercorns, lightly crushed

350 g/12 oz steak, sliced into long strips, 1–2cm/½–¾ inch wide

vegetable oil, for deep-frying

In a large bowl, mix the *nam pla*, whisky (if using), soy and sugar, and stir through the crushed pepper. Marinate the steak strips in the mixture for at least 1 hour, preferably overnight, in the refrigerator.

At this point, you can dry the beef on a rack in a very low oven – we're talking 50°C/125°F – for 1 hour, turning halfway through. Or, if you're impatient like me, you can skip ahead to the frying.

Heat the oil in a wok over a medium-high heat. Fry the beef strips in batches until crisp and mahogany, setting them aside to drain on paper towels as you go.

Serve with Sriracha sauce or either *Nam Jim Jaew* (Roasted Chilli Dipping Sauce, page 194) on the side.

~ If you like, you can slice 3–4 kaffir lime leaves into slivers and deep-fry them before you cook the beef. This slightly flavours the oil, and they make a tasty counterpoint to the neua dat deow. ~

~ If you add a teaspoon of coriander seed when you crush the peppercorns, the dish becomes neua sawan, or 'heavenly' beef. ~

~ You can substitute the beef for pork to make moo dat deow. ~

It Ain't Street Food If It Ain't On The Street...

There seems to be an urban myth that the best type of Thai food is street food.
It is not. It's just one type of Thai food. It is cheap, quick and often relies on the
skill of someone who has been cooking the same one dish for 40 years.

Cooking street food is a discipline apart from cheffing or home cooking,
so please – don't expect to be able to replicate it in your kitchen at home.
For one thing, regular gas hobs/stove tops cannot achieve that fierce, live fire
heat of the vendor who has been up since the crack of dawn tending his coals.

You can't…

So don't try to.

Instead, make the most honest and delicious dish you can. Sit down at your table,
or on a blanket in the garden, and enjoy it with a cold refreshment. And plan
a street-food-eating tour next time you're in Thailand.

Seua Rong Hai

'Crying Tiger'

This is simply rare grilled steak with a very fiery dip. So, why is it called 'crying tiger'? Well... (as my Irish grandmother might say) once upon a time, some villagers were preparing a feast. Among the many dishes, they planned to serve this. However, as the steak rested in the cool shade beside its sauce, it was smelled by a passing tiger. Much like the tiger who came to tea, this tiger was very, very hungry. It snuck into the village right up to the steak and devoured it, sauce and all. But the sauce was very, very hot. So hot, it burned the tiger's mouth. It shrieked in pain. What a commotion! And the villagers came running just in time to see the poor tiger running away, crying.

The dipping sauce, the *Nam Jim Jaew* (Roasted Chilli Dipping Sauce, page 194) , isn't actually that hot – just enough to get the juices flowing.

Serves 2–4

400 g/14 oz sirloin or rib-eye steak

1 tbsp soy sauce

1 tsp vegetable oil

Nam Jim Jaew (Roasted Chilli Dipping Sauce, page 194), to serve

Marinate the steak in the soy sauce and vegetable oil for 15 minutes or so.

Heat a grill (broiler) pan, or a barbecue (outdoor grill) until it's properly hot.

Slap on the steak and grill (broil) it to your liking – about 5–6 minutes for rare, no more than 8 minutes all-in for medium. Set it aside to rest for another 5–10 minutes.

Meanwhile, make up the *Nam Jim Jaew*. (You may want to double the quantity.)

Slice the steak thinly and serve on a plate alongside the dipping sauce.

Three Things On Sticks

The Stick Man on Soi Saladaeng sells one of my favourite street-food snacks in the world – grilled pork, chicken and chicken livers… on sticks. I call him Stick Man because his stall is always so busy, I've never had time to ask his name, let alone have a bit of a chat. But that's hardly surprising because his sticks are so damned good, and the perfect thing to have with a drink, or with *Som Tum Thai* (Green Papaya Salad, page 174) and sticky rice for a quick lunch. The marinade here isn't his – the lack of time to chat has seen to that – but it's as close as I've been able to get.

Makes approx. 12 sticks

400 g/14 oz pork shoulder (butt),
  or boneless chicken thigh,
  or chicken livers
Nam Jim Jaew (Roasted Chilli Dipping
  Sauce, page 194), to serve

for the marinade
2 coriander (cilantro) roots
  (see page 203)
1 garlic clove
½ tsp white peppercorns (optional)
2 tbsp *nam pla* (fish sauce)
1 tbsp palm sugar
2 tbsp oyster sauce

you will also need
wooden satay sticks or skewers,
  soaked in cold water

First, prepare the pork or chicken meat by trimming away any excess fat and cutting it into 2.5-cm/1-inch cubes. Prepare the chicken livers by separating the lobes and trimming away the nasty bits.

To make the marinade, pound together the coriander root and garlic, with the peppercorns (if using), in a pestle and mortar until you have a paste. Then, stir in the remaining ingredients until well combined. If you are planning to make all three kinds of sticks at once, you will need to make three separate batches of it.

Marinate the meat for at least 1 hour in the refrigerator.

Heat a charcoal grill to medium.

When you're ready to cook, thread the meat on to the sticks – no more than 4–6 pieces per stick. Grill the sticks over the coals for about 10 minutes until cooked through.

Alternatively, heat a griddle (grill) pan on your stove top, again to medium, and cook on all sides until cooked through.

Serve with the *Nam Jim Jaew* on the side.

Rice
and
Noodles

It is the neutral maypole
at the centre of the
table, around which all
other flavours dance.
It fills the stomach and
feeds the soul. It is as
constant and dependable
as the summer rains.

On Rice

Of all the things my mother left me when she died, perhaps the most precious to me is her rice bowl. Made of heavy blue and white china, it holds a thousand memories. And, with its sturdy lid, it never fails to deliver that set-piece moment of any Thai meal: the moment when the lid comes off and the scented steam of jasmine rice perfumes the air with the promise of the feast to come.

Rice is central to Southeast Asian food. Each country in the region has its own particular relationship with it. It is the neutral maypole at the centre of the table around which all other flavours dance. It fills the stomach and feeds the soul. It is as constant and dependable as the summer rains.

Rice is so key to Thai food that you don't ask your friends if they've had dinner yet, you ask *'Tarn khao ayang?'* or *'Bai kin khao ma?'* ('Have you had rice yet?' or 'Do you want to get some rice?'). Why? Because — and this may perhaps be the most important thing that foreigners don't understand about Thai food — rice is not a side dish. It is the *main* dish. Everything else on the table, no matter how fiery, feisty or delicious, is an accompaniment.

Rice has so profoundly shaped Thailand and its people that it is revered at every stage of life. It is at the heart of Thai customs and culture, integral to the celebration of births, marriages and deaths, scattered across the floor at a cremation to separate the living from the dead.

Its very cultivation has transformed the landscape from virgin forest to vibrant, verdant paddy fields, filled with life-giving grains of rice. Not to mention a host of fish and frogs and birds that can be captured and transformed into sustenance.

No wonder, then, that Thais cherish so many myths about the grain that feeds their entire way of life. Rice has a soul, a *khwan*. Observances must be made to ensure its untroubled growth. For it is a gift from the animist gods, and each region of the country has a tale of its own of how rice came to feed the nation.

As a Thai-born girl with a foreign face, I often wonder if my love of rice is the most obviously Thai thing about me. Certainly, when I move to a new place, Thai rice is one of the first things I cook because the scent of it (and fish sauce) smells of home. And I would never dream of cooking anything other than a Thai rice to serve with Thai food. As delicious as basmati is, with Thai food it's just plain wrong.

I say 'Thai rice' because, although *hom mali* or jasmine rice is the most famous and readily available Thai varietal, there are many others, grown all across the country. Brown, red, black, white, all can be found. Indeed, some restaurants now pride themselves on serving you options between them.

One of my particular favourites comes from the island of Koh Klang, which lies just off Krabi. Here, the local sangyod rice strain not only survives but thrives in slightly brackish paddies, the salinity of the water giving the grains a subtly different taste, all the better to pair with the crashing, banging, fierceness of southern Thai flavours.

So, please, don't just smother your rice with curry sauce. Savour each grain. Engage with it as the true star of your Thai meal. Rice is your friend, your ally, and the best thing to take away the blistering burn of chilli.

How To Cook Rice

I'm biased, I know, but I think Thai *hom mali* – jasmine rice – is the best in the world. It's fragrant and delicious, and its texture is second to none.

I cook it 'by the measure' in a pot with a good lid over the gas hob. Unless I'm cooking for a lot of people, when I'll use a rice cooker, because I don't have the hob space or I don't have a big enough pot. What's brilliant about 'by the measure' is that, if there's just two of us and we're not that hungry, I might use a coffee cup to measure out the rice. If one of the nephews or nieces has brought an extra chum, I can make two mugfuls in a larger pot. I can use two again if I want to make extra for a Fried Rice (page 45) or a Khao Tom (Rice Soup, page 43) tomorrow. It doesn't matter, because it always works. The only variable you have to look out for is the age of your rice: the older the rice, the drier it is, so you might need to add a little more water.

1 measure of jasmine rice
1⅓ measure of cold water

First, rinse the rice in a sieve (strainer) under cold running water, until some of the starch has run off.

Pour the rice and the measured water into a saucepan or casserole which has a tight-fitting lid. Place over the heat and bring to the boil. As soon as it's boiling, turn the heat right down to a simmer and pop the lid on. Cook for about 10–12 minutes.

When the time's up, taste it. If it's not quite cooked, add a dash more water and cook for a little longer. You should be able to smell when it's done – its wonderful perfume fills the kitchen.

Turn off the heat and let it rest for at least 5–10 minutes, so each individual grain of rice can puff up to its perfect glory. It will happily sit and keep warm for up to 30 minutes, leaving you plenty of time to pull everything else together.

~ *As a general guideline, allow about 75 g/3 oz uncooked rice per person.* ~

How To Cook Sticky Rice

Sticky rice (*khao niao*) is the staple in Isaan and Laos. It comes to the table in one large or several individual lidded baskets (*kradip khao niao*), wrapped in banana leaf or, more commonly these days, clingfilm (plastic wrap). It's also (unappealingly) known as glutinous rice. If that in any way worries you, please note that this does not mean it contains gluten, just that it's sticky, a quality caused by a selected mutation that means it has a very high quotient of amylopectin.

Traditional sticky rice is cooked in a special steaming basket that sits over a pear-shaped vessel of boiling water. The rice is turned in the basket about three quarters of the way through cooking, to ensure it all steams evenly. Most of us don't have such things, so it's easiest to cook it in a steamer.

1 measure of sticky rice

Soak one measure of sticky rice (say, a mugful) in a bowl of cold water for 3 hours. Drain, and rinse the rice in fresh water.

Bring water to the boil in the base of a steamer. Place the soaked and rinsed rice in a clean muslin (cheesecloth), and place that in the steamer's upper level. Make sure the rice, in its muslin, is spread in an even layer. Steam the rice, covered, for about 20 minutes. When it's done, the rice should be soft and sticky, but not mushy.

Divide into portions and serve.

You can also make it in a microwave. Soak the rice for 15–20 minutes in cold water, then rinse until the water runs clear. Place the rice in a microwave-safe bowl, and cook on high for 3 minutes. Remove from the microwave, stir the rice, then cook again for another 3 minutes or so. The rice should look translucent, and feel as above. If it doesn't, stir again, give it another couple of minutes, and you're done.

~ Rice generally doubles in size when cooked, so 125 g (4 oz) uncooked makes approximately 250 g (9 oz) cooked, which is enough for 2–4 people when served alongside other dishes. ~

Khao Tom

Rice Soup

This is a distinctly Thai soup that is at once both profoundly soothing and the most excellent breakfast. It's also a very good way of using up the rice left over from the night before.

You can use either the Basic Pork or Chicken Stock (page 86) for this, or powdered stocks to make life simple. You can also substitute the pork for chicken, or you can make the whole thing vegetarian using mushrooms, a vegetable stock and the Vegan Fish Sauce (page 192).

If you're using a store-bought stock or stock powder, taste it for saltiness.

Serves 2

2 tbsp vegetable oil

2 garlic cloves, chopped

500 ml/17½ fl oz/2 cups stock
   (see above)

250 g/9 oz/2⅓ cups cooked jasmine rice
   (125 g/4½ oz/⅔ cup uncooked rice)

80 g/2¾ oz minced (ground) pork

1 tbsp *nam pla* (fish sauce)

1 tbsp light soy sauce

a good pinch of sugar

to garnish

1 spring onion (scallion), finely sliced

1 tbsp fresh coriander (cilantro) leaves

2.5-cm/1-inch piece of fresh ginger,
   peeled and finely slivered

a good grinding of white pepper

1 tbsp preserved radish (optional)

1 salted egg, halved (optional)

Heat the oil in a saucepan, and fry the garlic until it's golden and fragrant. Set aside to cool and allow the garlic to infuse into the oil.

In a larger saucepan, bring the stock to the boil and add the rice. Add the pork by pinching off small pieces into the liquid until you have used all of it. Bring back to the boil, add the *nam pla*, soy sauce and sugar and simmer gently until the pork is cooked.

Divide into two bowls, scatter the fried garlic over the top, along with a drizzle of its oil, and garnish with the spring onion, white pepper, ginger and coriander, and the preserved radish and salted egg, if using.

Serve with a *Kruang Poong* (page 192) on the side.

Khao Pad Goong

Fried Rice with Prawns

Fried rice is one of the great comfort dishes – it's filling, soothing and satisfying. I've used prawns in this version, but you can use slivered beef, pork, chicken, tofu, whatever. Feel free to pull back the chilli, too, if you like. You can always add extra heat later with some *Nam Pla Prik* (Fish Sauce with Chillies, page 193).

Three words of cooking caution: firstly, when you add the rice, you may be tempted to add more oil. Don't do it. It will make the dish claggy. Keep breaking up the rice as you stir it through the wok, and work through it. Secondly, if you want to make this for more than two, by all means do. But don't double up all the ingredients and throw it all into one wok. Make the dish once, wipe out your wok, and go again with the second batch. Thirdly, make sure the cooked rice is at room temperature when you make this. If it's too warm and steamy, it will clump and stick. If it's too cold, it will turn out as hard as a rock.

Serves 2

2 tbsp vegetable oil

2 garlic cloves, peeled and finely chopped

180 g/6 oz peeled prawns (shrimp)

2–3 Thai bird's eye chillies, chopped

1 tbsp *nam pla* (fish sauce)

1 tbsp light soy sauce

a good pinch of sugar

500 g/1 lb 2 oz/4½ cups cooked rice (about 240 g/8½ oz/1⅓ cups uncooked rice)

½ onion, peeled and finely sliced

1 spring onion (scallion), green part only, sliced

a good grinding of white pepper

fresh coriander (cilantro) leaves, to garnish

cucumber slices, to serve

lime wedges, to serve

Heat the wok or frying pan (skillet) until it's very hot. Add the oil, then the garlic and stir-fry until golden. Add the prawns and the chillies, and carry on stirring, adding the *nam pla*, soy sauce and sugar, until the prawns are cooked. Add the cooked rice and stir through well, breaking up any clumps. Add the onion and the spring onion and incorporate well. Season with white pepper, then turn on to plates and serve sprinkled with coriander and with the cucumber slices and lime wedges on the side.

Serve with *Kai Dao* (Deep-fried Eggs, page 133) on the top and *Nam Pla Prik* (Fish Sauce with Chillies, page 193), as pictured, on the side.

Khao Mun Gai

Thai-Hunanese Chicken and Rice

This is one of my favourite Thai breakfasts. The chicken and rice are fragrant and soothing, while the *nam jim* is zingy and punchy. It's well worth cooking from scratch, but it's also a great way to use up leftover roast chicken, so I include both versions here.

My *nam jim* recipe is compiled from several versions I've had up and down the country, including the one from my favourite stall on Soi Saladaeng in Bangkok, run by my friend Khun Udonsak.

Serves 4–6

1 chicken, about 1.5 kg/3 lb 5 oz (there will be leftovers)

1 small onion, peeled and cut into chunks

4 coriander (cilantro) roots (see page 203), crushed

1 garlic clove, crushed

a good pinch of sea salt

a good grinding of white pepper

for the rice

1 tbsp vegetable oil

1–2 garlic cloves, peeled and finely chopped

275 g/9¾ oz/1½ cups jasmine rice, rinsed

for the *nam jim*

4-cm/1½-inch piece of fresh ginger, peeled and finely sliced

2–3 Thai bird's eye chillies, sliced

a small handful of fresh coriander (cilantro), chopped

2 tbsp yellow bean sauce

2 tbsp rice vinegar

2 tsp sugar

1 tbsp light soy sauce

1 tbsp dark soy sauce

to garnish

4-cm/1½-inch piece of cucumber, sliced

1 tbsp fresh coriander (cilantro) leaves

Put the chicken, onion, coriander root and garlic in a heavy-based stock pot or casserole and pour over cold water to cover. Season with salt and white pepper. Bring to the boil, then turn down to a very low simmer until the chicken is cooked, about 1 hour 20 minutes, depending on the size of the chicken. Skim off any scum on the surface of the water with a spoon. To test when it's done, remove the bird from the broth and insert a skewer or a fork into the thickest part of its thigh – if the juices run clear, not pinky-red, it's done. Set aside.

Strain the broth, then taste and adjust the seasoning accordingly. It should be very mild and soothing. Set aside to cool.

Next, cook the rice: heat the vegetable oil in a saucepan that has a tight-fitting lid. Gently fry the chopped garlic without letting it brown. Add the rice and stir to thoroughly coat in the oil. Cover the rice with 330 ml/ 11 fl oz/1⅓ cups of the cold broth, and bring it to the boil on a medium heat. When it starts to bubble, put the lid on the pan, turn the heat right down, and cook for 10–12 minutes. Taste to see if it's cooked – if it's not quite ready, add a dash more broth and cook for a little longer. Sometimes the age of the rice will affect its cooking time,

so keep an eye on it. Let the rice rest for 5–10 minutes before serving.

In a separate pan, bring the remaining broth to a simmer.

Meanwhile, make the *nam jim*: grind the ginger to a paste in a pestle and mortar. Add the chillies and coriander, stir together, then thoroughly combine with the other ingredients and 2 tbsp of the chicken broth. Spoon out into a communal serving bowl.

When ready to serve, slice the chicken and lay each portion beside a serving of rice. Garnish with the cucumber and coriander leaves and accompany with a small bowl of broth and the *nam jim*.

The Leftovers Method:

Make the broth from your chicken carcass, as though you were making stock. Then use your cold, roast chicken in place of the poached chicken. Everything else remains the same.

~ To serve the rice, I usually pack it into a small bowl (about 9 cm/3½ inches in diameter) and turn it out on to a plate to create each single serving, as you'll see in the photograph. ~

A good bowl
of noodle soup
is probably
one of the
world's greatest
breakfasts.

On Noodles

Although you find noodles all over Thailand, not least in the form of the ubiquitous *pad Thai*, they actually come from China, and most probably arrived in Thailand with Chinese traders at some point in the eighteenth century. Now they're everywhere: in soups, in curries, in stir-fries. In fact, a good bowl of noodle soup is probably one of the world's greatest breakfasts.

Rice noodles (*guay teow*) are made from an unleavened dough of rice flour and water. They come in wide ribbons (*sen yai*) and thin (*sen lek*), and whichever you use is generally up to you. In soups, they are interchangeable. Then there's *sen mee*, the thin vermicelli noodles that are almost always sold dried.

Egg noodles (*ba mee*) can also be used interchangeably in noodle soups.

And there's *kanom jeen*, a uniquely Thai style of noodle, which probably originated with the Mon people, who lived in central Thailand before the Tai ethnic group migrated south. Here, the noodles are made with fermented rice.

While you can, sometimes, find all of the above styles of noodle sold freshly made in Asian supermarkets, you will most likely have to make do with dried. Each brand cooks slightly differently, so always follow the instructions on the packet.

I've kept the noodle recipes fairly straightforward here, primarily because there are so many minor regional variations on the basic themes that I could've ended up with a whole book on noodles wherein all the recipes looked broadly the same. These are the ones I make at home. With the exception of *pad Thai*, which I only ever seem to cook on request or when I'm teaching, because – if I'm going to go to that much trouble – I'd rather make something else. So sue me.

Pad Thai

This is probably the most requested dish in the Thai repertoire. So perhaps, for once, we should call it by its proper name: *Guay Teow Pad Thai*, or 'noodles stir-fried in the Thai style'.

How it came to be so widespread across Thailand is down to Prime Minister Plaek Phibunsongkhram, more commonly known as Phibun, who came to power in 1938. Very conscious of protecting Siam's (as it was then) independence, he passed 12 Cultural Mandates between 1938 and 1942 in a bid to turn Thailand (he renamed it) into a proud and modern country.

In the process, he ordered the creation of a new national dish. Restaurants across the country were given the recipe; anyone with the inclination to open a *pad Thai* street-food stall was provided with state help to do so; and it was cheap. Small wonder that it quickly became so popular.

A good *pad Thai* is all about the preparation. There is a lot to do before you fire up your wok and assemble the dish. Fortunately, none of it is especially difficult, just time consuming. So, make sure you have everything prepared and in easy reach before the final cooking.

Serves 2

4 tbsp vegetable oil

1 tbsp dried prawns (shrimp)

125 g/4½ oz medium rice noodles

1 tbsp palm sugar

1 tbsp *nam pla* (fish sauce)

1 tbsp tamarind paste (purée)

1 tbsp unsalted peanuts, roasted
    (see tip)

juice of ½ lime

4 garlic cloves, peeled and
    finely chopped

200 g/7 oz raw peeled prawns (shrimp)

2 eggs, lightly beaten

75 g/2½ oz beansprouts

100 g/3½ oz firm tofu, cut into
    1-cm/½-inch cubes

1 tbsp preserved radish, finely chopped
    (optional)

to garnish

a small handful of garlic chives or
    2 spring onions (scallions), green
    parts only, sliced

a handful of unsalted peanuts, roasted
    (see tip)

a handful of beansprouts

a little fresh chopped coriander
    (cilantro)

to serve

cucumber slices

lime wedges

Heat 2 tablespoons of the vegetable oil in a wok. When it's very hot, add the dried prawns and stir-fry them until they are crisp and lightly golden. This should take no more than 30 seconds–1 minute. Remove with a slotted spoon to paper towels to cool.

Meanwhile, prepare the noodles according to the packet instructions. Drain and refresh in cold water. Set aside to dry.

While the noodles soften, make the sauce: gently heat the palm sugar, *nam pla* and the tamarind paste with a splash of water in a small saucepan, stirring until the sugar dissolves. Remove from the heat and set aside.

Pound the dried prawns and the peanuts loosely in a pestle and mortar – you just want an amalgamation, not a paste.

Now, check through the ingredient list once again: make sure you've done all the prep. Once the wok's on the heat, there's no turning back! Add the lime juice to the sauce, and you're all set.

Heat the remaining 2 tablespoons of oil in a wok over the highest possible heat. Add the garlic and stir until it is just fragrant. Add the raw prawns, and stir-fry until they are pink and cooked. Add the beaten eggs, swirling them around the wok, then quickly add the noodles, the peanut and shrimp mixture, the beansprouts, tofu, preserved radish (if using) and the sauce.
Stir it together rapidly, making sure it is well combined, then turn out on to plates.

Garnish with the garlic chives or spring onion greens, extra peanuts, beansprouts and chopped coriander and serve immediately, accompanied by sliced cucumber, wedges of fresh lime and the *Kruang Poong* (page 192).

~ To roast the peanuts, scatter them on a baking tray and bake them in a low oven for about 5–8 minutes, shaking the tray a couple of times, until they are golden brown. Remove and set aside on paper towels until you need them. ~

Pad Kee Mao

'Drunkard's Noodles'

So called, because it's alleged to be an excellent hangover cure, better even than a bacon sandwich. Most often, you'll find this served with beef (as here in the photograph), but it is equally delicious with pork or chicken, depending on what you have around. You can substitute the noodles for the same amount of cold cooked rice (added at the same time as you would add the noodles) to make *khao pad kee mao*... in which case, be sure to serve it with a deep-fried egg (page 133) on top.

Serves 2

115 g/4 oz *sen yai* (large) rice noodles

1 heaped tsp *nam prik pao* (roasted chilli paste, see page 203)

1 tbsp dark soy sauce

2 tbsp *nam pla* (fish sauce)

1 tsp tamarind paste (purée)

1 tsp chilli powder

a pinch of sugar

2–3 Thai bird's eye chillies

2 garlic cloves, peeled

2 coriander (cilantro) roots (see page 203)

a pinch of salt

2 tbsp vegetable oil

125 g/4½ oz beef, pork or chicken, cut into thin strips

1 tomato, cut into 8 wedges

4 kaffir lime leaves, finely sliced

a large handful of Thai basil leaves, plus extra to garnish

In a large bowl, soak the noodles in hot water until they separate and reach the texture of uncooked fresh pasta.

In a small bowl, mix together the *nam prik pao*, dark soy, *nam pla,* tamarind paste, chilli powder and sugar, until the sugar has dissolved.

Pound the chillies, garlic and coriander root together with the salt in a pestle and mortar until you have a rough paste.

Heat your wok over a high heat until it's very hot, then add the oil. Add the garlic and coriander root paste, and stir-fry for a minute or so until it's really fragrant, then add the meat. Stir-fry until it takes colour, then add the tomato, lime leaves and the chilli paste mixture, stirring them in well. Now add the drained noodles and half of the basil. Keep stir-frying until everything is cooked through and well combined, about 5 minutes. Stir through the remaining basil and serve immediately, garnished with the extra basil leaves.

Guay Teow Nahm

A Simple Noodle Soup

Guay Teow Nahm is not a dish to sweat over. This is grab-a-seat-at-a-stall-and-it-will-be-in-front-of-you-in-minutes food. So let's be frank: what you make at home won't taste anything like what you buy on the street. Those guys have been making that stock for that soup for generations. Don't try to compare this to that.

This is a quick breakfast or lunch that you can have ready in 30 minutes. If you have the time, make the Basic Pork Stock (page 86). Failing that, I often use chicken stock made from the Sunday leftovers or a Thai pork stock powder, which you can buy at most Asian supermarkets. It all depends on what I have in when the mood for noodles strikes.

This version is made with rice noodles (*guay teow*). If you make it with egg noodles, it becomes *Ba Mee Nahm*.

Serves 2 greedy souls or 4 daintier appetites

90 g/3¼ oz medium-width dried
    rice noodles

2 garlic cloves

2 coriander (cilantro) roots
    (see page 203), roughly chopped

a pinch of salt

1 tbsp vegetable oil

750 ml/1¼ pints/3 cups stock

1 tbsp light soy sauce, or to taste

1½ tbsp *nam pla* (fish sauce),
    or to taste

200 g/7 oz pork or chicken,
    thinly sliced

100 g/3½ oz pak choi (bok choy) or
    pak boong (Siamese watercress),
    roughly chopped

a handful of beansprouts

to garnish

3 spring onions (scallions), trimmed
    and finely sliced

fresh coriander (cilantro) leaves

sweet basil leaves (optional)

deep-fried garlic (see page 204)
    (optional)

Prepare the noodles by soaking them in a large bowl of very hot water, as per the instructions on the packet. This softens them and removes excess starch, which will make the soup gummy. Times may vary – you want a malleable noodle, not a squishy one – the texture of fresh pasta. Drain, rinse with cold water and set aside.

Meanwhile, pound the garlic and the coriander root together in a pestle and mortar with a pinch of salt.

Heat the oil in a saucepan, then add the garlic and coriander root paste. Cook until fragrant but not coloured, then add the stock. Bring it up to the boil, add the soy and *nam pla*, followed by the pork or chicken. Simmer until the meat is cooked through, a minute or two, then add the pak choi or *pak boong*. Bring back to the boil, and cook for another minute, until the vegetables are cooked but retain some bite. Taste the broth

and adjust the seasoning – you may need a little more soy or *nam pla*.

Divide the noodles between the bowls. Add the beansprouts. Ladle the soup over the top, and garnish with the spring onion, coriander, sweet basil and deep-fried garlic, if using. Serve straight away with a *Kruang Poong* (page 192) on the side.

~ *You can add ¼ tsp white peppercorns to the mortar when you pound the garlic and coriander root, if you like.* ~

~ *If you have any leftover cooked chicken, pork or steak, you can exchange it for the raw meat. Just add the cooked leftovers at the end with the beansprouts.* ~

Ba Mee Haeng

'Dry' Egg Noodles

Ba Mee Haeng is, simply, the opposite of *Ba Mee Nam*. The latter is a noodle soup, and so is the former... without the soup.

I've designed this to use up leftover pork. With barbecued pork, this is a phenomenon that rarely happens, but I often find I have roast pork leftovers, which work very well. And if I have none, I'll buy Chinese barbecued pork, which the Thais call *moo dang*, or red pork, in Chinatown.

I also often make this with packets of Thai instant noodles – Mama is my preferred brand – which I always have in the cupboard. I'll often make *Ba Mee Nam* with them too, and, if I'm feeling extra indulgent, I'll poach an egg in the stock alongside them for added silky richness.

Serves 2

2 garlic cloves, finely chopped and deep-fried (page 204)

2 tsp caster (superfine) sugar

2 tbsp *nam pla* (fish sauce)

1 pak choi (bok choy), halved and sliced

100 g/3½ oz beansprouts

2 nests dried egg noodles

160 g/5½ oz barbecued pork, thinly sliced

2 tbsp pickled mustard greens

2 spring onions (scallions), green parts only, finely sliced

1 tbsp coriander (cilantro) leaves

First, deep-fry the garlic and set aside reserving 2 tablespoons of its frying oil. Then dissolve the sugar in the *nam pla*, and set aside.

Bring a large saucepan of water to the boil. Blanch the pak choi and divide it equally between two bowls. Then blanch the beansprouts and divide between the bowls. Finally, cook the noodles according to the instructions on the packet and divide them between the bowls.

Top the bowls equally with the remaining ingredients, and serve with lime wedges and a *Kruang Poong* (Page 192) on the side.

~ *Don't be snobbish about packets of instant dried noodles like the ones from Mama – most Thais (including me) grew up on the stuff. My suitcase back to boarding schools was stuffed with them... and fish sauce. Pimp them up with any vegetables you have lying around, leftovers bits of meat or ham, pickled mustard greens, a spoon or two of kim chi or yellow bean sauce, an egg. They're delicious. And super quick to make.* ~

Kow Soi

Chiang Mai Curried Noodles

This may be one of my most beloved examples of Thai home cooking. It's my Dad's recipe, and *kow soi* was his favourite dish.

When I had just turned seven, my Mum returned to England to put my sister into school. So Dad took me with him on a trip to Chiang Mai. It was my first time in the north, and I loved it. But my abiding memory is not of elephants and farmers and golden temples; it's of going to a *kow soi* restaurant, where Dad ate so many bowls of it he had to be taken back to the hotel in a wheelbarrow. A stunt that, in retrospect, I realise was more for my amusement than necessity. But still.

When they retired to Gozo, he and Mum would cook Thai food at least once a week, adapting recipes as best they could with the ingredients they could find. And I was tasked with carting suitcases full of their favourite brand of curry paste each time I visited, which left my swimwear with an interesting aroma.

Even as a widower, Dad would make a batch of this once a month, freezing the portions so that he could have it every Sunday.

The recipe demonstrates a typical Thai home cook's trick: paste adaptation. Rather than filling your fridge with every kind of paste, or making it from scratch every time, you simply add the missing spices, often in powdered form, either to the paste or the developing curry; which is incredibly practical, when you think about it.

Serves 4–6

Recipe continues overleaf.

2 tbsp vegetable oil

4 garlic cloves, finely chopped

4 heaped tbsp good-quality red curry paste

2 x 400-ml/14-fl oz cans of coconut milk

800 ml/27 fl oz/scant 3½ cups chicken stock

650 g/1½ lb chicken thighs, cut into 2-cm/¾-inch pieces

1 heaped tsp ground turmeric

3 tbsp hot curry powder

2 long dried red chillies

2½ tbsp *nam pla* (fish sauce)

1 tsp fresh lime juice

65–70 g/2¼–2½ oz egg noodles per head (about a 'nest' each), uncooked weight

to garnish

crispy egg noodles (see tip)

4 Thai shallots or 2 regular shallots, peeled and sliced

lime wedges

extra *nam pla* (fish sauce)

nam prik pao (roasted chilli paste, see page 203)

fermented mustard greens (see tip)

In a large saucepan, heat the oil over a medium-high heat until hot. Add the garlic and stir-fry until golden brown, then add the curry paste and stir-fry until fragrant — no more than 30 seconds–1 minute. Add half of the coconut milk and stir gently until the paste dissolves into it. Then add the rest of the coconut milk and the stock, and allow to bubble gently until the sauce starts to reduce and to thicken slightly.

Add the chicken, stirring it into the sauce. Then add the turmeric, curry powder, dried chillies, *nam pla* and lime juice, stirring them in well. Turn down the heat, and simmer until the chicken is cooked, about 20 minutes.

Meanwhile, prepare the noodles according to the packet instructions. Drain, then place each portion of noodles into a bowl.

Spoon the curry generously over the top of the noodles and serve with the garnish ingredients on the side.

~ This is quite a spicy, heat-forward version. If you prefer a milder, creamier taste, just stir in some coconut cream on the final heat-through. ~

~ To make the crispy egg noodle garnish, soak a coil or two of egg noodles as per packet instructions. Drain and dry them well on some paper towel. Heat some oil for deep-frying. Gently lower the noodles a handful at a time into the hot oil and gently fry until crisp, turning with tongs. Remove from the oil and drain on fresh paper towels. Then, fry each batch again until they turn golden. Drain well and serve on top of the Kow Soi. ~

~ Fermented mustard greens can be found in cans or vacuum packs in most Asian supermarkets. Use any left over chopped up and stirred into a Kai Jeow (Thai Omelette, page 134). ~

Kanom Jeen Khun Oot

Khun Oot's Pork Noodles from Mae Hong Son

Kanom Jeen is a popular street-food dish all over Thailand. It's made with cooked, cold noodles served with a hot sauce over the top. This one, which I discovered at Khun Oot's stall in Mae Hong Son market, is halfway between a Thai *kanom jeen* and a Lao *kow soi*. It makes for the best breakfast!

Some key things: first, this derives from a Shan dish, so there's no *nam pla* here. Second, it's often served with *ngiaw* flowers, dried blossoms from the red cotton tree. They're hard to find outside of Thailand, so I don't use them. Third, the *kanom jeen* noodles are very specific. They're a fermented rice noodle. In Thailand you can buy them fresh; elsewhere, you cannot. I favour No.1 Hand Brand, a Thai product you can find in most good Asian supermarkets. Do substitute a good-quality rice noodle if you cannot find them.

Serves 2 'fat *farang*' or 4 normal people

100 g/3½ oz dried *kanom jeen* noodles

3 Thai shallots or 1 regular shallot, peeled and chopped

3 garlic cloves, peeled and chopped

4–6 Thai bird's eye chillies

2 dried bird's eye (bird) chillies

a good pinch of salt

2 tbsp vegetable oil

200 g/7 oz minced (ground) pork

4 good, ripe small tomatoes or 8 cherry tomatoes, chopped

2 tsp *kapi* (shrimp paste)

600 ml/1 pint/2½ cups chicken or pork stock

2 tsp palm sugar

1–2 tsp light soy sauce

1 tbsp tomato purée (paste), if necessary

to serve

2 good handfuls of beansprouts

2 spring onions (scallions), chopped

crispy rice noodles (optional)

lime wedges

roasted chilli powder (available in Asian supermarkets)

Kap Moo (Pork Scratchings, page 128)

First prepare the noodles as per the instructions on the packet, then drain and allow them to go cold. You can do this well ahead of time.

Pound the shallots, garlic and chillies in a pestle and mortar along with a pinch of salt until you have a paste.

Heat the oil in a wok and fry off the paste until fragrant, this will only take about 30 seconds–1 minute. Add the pork and the tomatoes and keep on stir-frying until everything has amalgamated and the pork is cooked. Add the *kapi* and stir through until it's well mixed in. Add the stock, sugar and soy sauce, stir through and bring back to the boil. Taste: you want it salty, sweet and sharp from the tomatoes. Adjust the seasoning if you like, and add the tomato purée if your tomatoes are not up to scratch.

Divide the cold noodles between the bowls and pour over the sauce. Top with beansprouts, spring onions and crispy noodles, if using. Serve with lime wedges, roasted chilli powder, pork scratchings and extra beansprouts on the side.

NOV 72

Curries

On Thai Curries

In general terms, a Thai curry begins with a paste that is fried in a wok or saucepan before being dissolved into a liquid. Frequently, that liquid will be coconut milk; in the north and northeast, which is not coconut country, it will tend to be water.

So far, so straight-forward. But you will have noticed that I haven't told you what to fry the curry paste with. Most of the recipes that follow instruct you to use vegetable oil. This is not technically correct, though it is convenient.

The Thai convention for a curry made with coconut milk is to 'crack' coconut cream – the thick bit in an unshaken can of coconut milk, or the stuff sold separately. This is done by heating the coconut cream in your wok or saucepan to separate its water from its fat, which you will see happening. You then fry the paste in that fat. However, most commercial coconut milk and cream use emulsifiers to ensure their longevity, and these inhibit the 'cracking' process. Without access to the fresh stuff, we must a) make it ourselves (you will find a recipe to do just that on the opposite page); b) find a product without the preservatives and chemicals; or c) use something else, hence vegetable oil. Some may sneer, but I view it as a small sacrifice to make, and most people won't notice the difference.

The quality of coconut milk varies enormously from brand to brand. Even so, I always have a couple of cans in the cupboard, ideally without additives. Aroy D, a Thai brand, is excellent. Above all, avoid the dried blocks of coconut 'something'. They are abominable.

As for the pastes themselves, each recipe that follows will tell you how to make the one that's relevant. This does not mean that you have to every time. Most Thai home cooks buy their pastes in the market or supermarket.

If you can source all the ingredients, and you have the time and the inclination, make the paste, if only for the experience. If you find that you prefer the flavour of a fresh paste, as I do, build its making into your schedule. I'll often make pastes a day or two ahead of time, just to have one less thing to do when I finally cook. Don't worry if you can't be bothered: store-bought paste will work just fine.

Having said that, there are good pastes and not-so-good pastes. My favourite is the Nittaya brand. Next comes the Mae Ploy and Mae Pranom brands – they are all vacuum-packed rather than canned, which I prefer. When using one of these, replace my paste with 2 heaped tablespoons of bought. Better yet, go to Thailand, visit a market, and buy some fresh pastes. Many stalls have the wherewithal to vacuum-seal them for your trip home.

Making Your Own Coconut Milk

With a screwdriver and a mallet (and a willing helper), puncture the three eyes at the top of the nut. Drain out the water and discard it. Place the coconut on newspaper on the floor, and set about it with a hammer until it cracks open – I average about two solid blows.

Grate the coconut flesh away from the shell. The Thais have a handy tool for this, which allows you to hold the shell in one hand and grate away. If you don't have one, prise the meat away from the shell with an oyster knife and grate the flesh with a box-grater. This is a more wasteful process, because the curve of the coconut means the flesh will not be flush with the grater, and some will get left behind. But, as someone said, waddaya gonna do?

Soak the grated coconut in lukewarm to hot water (allow 230 ml/8 fl oz/scant 1 cup per coconut) and squeeze the milk out of the flesh by hand for a few minutes. Squeeze out the coconut over a sieve (strainer), reserving the milk in one bowl and the flesh in another, then repeat the process. Finally, strain both batches of coconut milk through muslin (cheesecloth) into another bowl. All in all, it should take you about 1 hour 15 minutes and yield about 1 litre/1¾ pints/4 cups of coconut milk. Once it has settled, the rich coconut cream will have risen to the top.

Gaeng Keow Wan Gai

A Classic Green Chicken Curry

How many times have you seen a green curry described as 'mild' or 'sweet'? It infuriates me, and I've seen it done a thousand times. And it isn't just Thai restaurants in Britain that do it. Several years ago, I took a boat down the river from Ayutthaya to Bangkok. As luck would have it, my husband and I were the only passengers and, after a long conversation with the crew, primarily about food, they promised to bin out the bland version they serve farang and to make it properly. And jolly good it was too: lively, fiery and delicious.

Part of the problem lies in how we translate the word *waan*. Generally, it means 'sweet'. In this case, it should really mean 'fresh'. This dish is all about bright, green flavours. The chlorophyll in the herbs should sing out like Maria Callas. This matter of freshness is the other reason for a poor green curry. Once the paste is made, it doesn't matter how many preservatives they use in it, the inherent green freshness will deteriorate quickly, so a store-bought *keow waan* paste will always disappoint.

This is the one curry paste you should always make from scratch. It's also the easiest, the best one to learn and practise on, and the best way to remember why the green curry became famous in the first place.

Serves 4

Recipe continues overleaf.

for the paste

½ tsp coriander seeds

½ tsp cumin seeds

1 tsp white peppercorns

a good pinch of salt

1 tbsp finely chopped galangal

1 tbsp finely chopped lemongrass

2 Thai shallots or 1 regular shallot, peeled and finely chopped

12 green Thai bird's eye chillies, de-stemmed and chopped

2 long green chillies, de-stemmed and finely chopped

4 tbsp finely chopped fresh coriander (cilantro) root (see tip), with some stem attached

1 garlic clove, peeled and finely chopped

2-cm/¾-inch piece of fresh turmeric, finely chopped

zest of 1 kaffir lime (see tip)

1 tsp *kapi* (shrimp paste)

for the curry

2 tbsp vegetable oil

1 x 400-ml/14-fl oz can of coconut milk

350 g/12 oz chicken thighs, cut into 2-cm/¾-inch dice

1–2 tbsp *nam pla* (fish sauce)

a pinch of caster (superfine) sugar (optional)

65 g/2¼ oz pea aubergines (eggplants)

2 Thai round aubergines (eggplants), cut into quarters

100 g/3½ oz bamboo shoots, chopped (see tip)

2 long red chillies, diagonally sliced into 3 pieces

a large handful of Thai sweet basil

1 long orange chilli (optional)

To make the paste: pound all the ingredients in a pestle and mortar (starting with hardest ingredients first, as listed, working down to the softest), until you have a uniform, close-textured paste. If it's not completely smooth, don't worry. If you prefer to use a food processor or a blender, again work from the hardest to the softest ingredients, and add about 1 tablespoon water or more to bring the paste together.

To make the curry: heat the oil in a wok or saucepan and fry the paste until it smells fragrant, about 1 minute. Add half of the coconut milk, bring to the boil slowly, stirring to dissolve the paste. Once the paste has dissolved, let the coconut milk simmer a little until you see oil appearing on the surface. Then add 200 ml/7 fl oz/scant 1 cup of water and bring to the boil.

Add the chicken and bring back to the boil, then add the rest of the coconut milk. Bring back to the boil and simmer for about 6 minutes. Add the *nam pla* and the sugar, if using. Taste and adjust the seasoning. If it seems a little thick, add a little more water – you want a soupiness, not a thick gravy.

Add the aubergines, the bamboo shoots and one of the long red chillies. Simmer for another 3 minutes or so. Taste – you want this to taste vibrant, hot, salty and herbaceous. Add the basil, the remaining red chilli and the whole orange chilli if you have one, and serve with some jasmine rice and *Nam Pla Prik* (Fish Sauce with Chillies, page 193).

~ Sometimes, you cannot find coriander root. If you can't, replace it with the same amount of coriander stem. It won't taste quite the same, and it will give you a greener curry, but it works very well. ~

~ If you cannot find kaffir limes, leave the zest out of the recipe altogether. ~

~ You can buy bamboo shoots either canned or vacuum-packed in water. I prefer the latter. You can easily find them in most Asian stores. If you can only find them canned, don't worry, they're perfectly good. ~

~ In Thailand, coconut milk comes with a thick cream. Traditionally, you'd fry your curry paste in this cream, adding the coconut milk when the cream 'cracks' and you can see its oil separate out. This oil, which should always appear on the top of a good Thai curry, adds a particular and special flavour. However, the emulsifiers added to a lot of canned coconut creams and milks often prevent this. So, in this recipe, I have fried-off the paste in vegetable oil, which works perfectly well. ~

~ If you want to make this with beef, which is very traditional, serve with Roti (page 71). ~

Note

No matter how many times you make this dish, the colour of the curry will vary. This is down to the quality and freshness of your ingredients. As the plants and fruits age, the green in their chlorophyll deteriorates. To punch up the green, add a few extra chopped coriander stems to the paste. A bit of a cheat, but it looks fabulous.

Gaeng Pet

Red Curry with Beef

There are several iterations of the classic Thai red curry; in fact, the red curry paste is one of the most adaptable in terms of using it as a standard template from which to create others. So here is the recipe for a basic *gaeng neua*, or beef red curry, just as Prayoon taught me to make it. And opposite, I tell you how to pimp it up into a *gaeng pet bpet*, or red curry with roast duck, which is a much fancier proposition.

Serves 4–6 as a part of a meal

for the paste

8–10 dried long red chillies

4 dried bird's eye (bird) chillies

1 tsp cumin seeds

1 tsp coriander seeds

1 tsp white peppercorns

2 tsp *kapi* (shrimp paste)

a pinch of salt

2 tbsp chopped galangal

4 tbsp chopped lemongrass

1 tbsp chopped coriander (cilantro) root (see page 203)

4 Thai shallots or 2 regular shallots, peeled and chopped

4 garlic cloves, peeled and chopped

zest of 1 kaffir lime

for the curry

2 tbsp vegetable oil

1 x 400-ml/14-fl oz can of coconut milk

1 tbsp *nam pla* (fish sauce), or more to taste

1 tsp caster (superfine) sugar, or more to taste

350 g/12 oz beef, cut into strips

a squeeze of lime juice, if necessary

100 g/3½ oz bamboo shoots (see tip on page 65)

3 kaffir lime leaves, torn

To make the paste: toast the dried chillies in a dry pan over a low heat for a few seconds, being careful not to burn them. Set aside to cool, then use a pair of scissors to cut off the stems and slit them lengthways. Scrape out and discard the seeds. Cut the chillies up into small pieces and soak in warm water for 20 minutes or until soft.

Meanwhile, toast the cumin seeds, coriander seeds and peppercorns in the same pan until fragrant, about 30 seconds–1 minute. Set aside.

Wrap the *kapi* in aluminium foil, and toast it in the dry pan for 1–2 minutes and set aside.

Pound the paste in a pestle and mortar, starting with the dried chillies and salt and working from the hardest to the softest ingredients, in the order listed. When you're done, it should be well amalgamated and pretty smooth.

To make the curry: heat the oil in a large saucepan, and fry off the curry paste until you can really smell it. Pour in half of the coconut milk, stirring it into the paste as it comes to the boil, until the paste is dissolved. Then add the rest of the coconut milk, along with 200 ml/7 fl oz/scant 1 cup water, the *nam pla* and sugar. Stir to incorporate. When the sauce comes back to the boil, add the beef and simmer until it's cooked, about 6–8 minutes. Taste, and adjust the seasoning. You may need to add a little more *nam pla* and sugar, and perhaps a squeeze of lime. Finally, add the bamboo shoots and the lime leaves and simmer for another 3–5 minutes. Serve with rice.

Gaeng Pet Bpet

Red Curry with Duck

This is a rather grander version of the red curry. You can roast some duck breast yourself for this, or you can simply buy some roast duck in your local Chinatown, and use about 350–400 g/ 12–14 oz of it instead. You can also replace the cherry tomatoes. Some people use pineapple or grapes, which I'm not so keen on. My friend Jao Fah adds lychees, which are delicious – use 8 here.

Serves 4–6

for the roast duck

2 duck breasts, skin on

2 tbsp dark soy sauce

1 tbsp caster (superfine) sugar

1 tsp Chinese five spice powder

for the curry

2 tbsp vegetable oil

1 quantity of curry paste (recipe opposite)

½ tsp ground cloves

½ tsp grated nutmeg

½ tsp ground turmeric

1 x 400-ml/14-fl oz can of coconut milk

1 tbsp *nam pla* (fish sauce)

1 tsp sugar

a squeeze of lime juice, if necessary

8–12 cherry tomatoes

3–4 kaffir lime leaves, torn

a handful of sweet basil

For the roast duck, marinate the duck breasts in the other ingredients for at least 30 minutes, or up to a couple of hours (in the refrigerator) if you have time.

Preheat the oven to 180°C fan/200°C/ 400°F/gas mark 6, and roast the duck on a baking tray, skin-side up, for 20–25 minutes for medium. Remove and set aside to rest and cool.

To make the curry: heat the oil in a large saucepan, and fry off the curry paste, along with the cloves, nutmeg and turmeric. Add half the coconut milk, stirring it into the paste to dissolve, and bring it back to the boil. Add the remaining coconut milk, 200 ml/7 fl oz/scant 1 cup water, *nam pla* and sugar and bring the sauce back to the boil, stirring to blend it together.

Slice the duck and add it to the curry. Taste and adjust the seasoning – you may need to add a little more sugar or *nam pla*, and perhaps some lime juice. Then add the tomatoes (or your chosen alternative) and lime leaves. Simmer for about 5 minutes, then add the basil and stir it in. Serve with rice.

Gaeng Kari Gai

Yellow Curry with Chicken and Potatoes

This is a mild, southern curry, rich and redolent of the Spice Route, and a simplified version of the one our cook Prayoon used to make every Saturday lunchtime. She would serve this with sliced banana, peanuts and cucumber pickle on the side, or with Bombay duck and salted egg.

Vegans and vegetarians should note that this is the one curry paste I make without shrimp paste, so have at it. You can substitute the fish sauce with soy or with the Vegan Fish Sauce on page 192.
In place of the chicken, use pumpkin or tofu or green papaya, or a mixture of the three. See the version opposite.

Serves 4 as a part of a meal

for the paste

8 long dried red chillies

seeds from 8 cardamom pods

1 tsp coriander seeds

2 tsp cumin seeds

1 tsp black peppercorns

a good pinch of salt

a pinch of mace

1 stick lemongrass, finely chopped

3–4-cm/1–1½-inch piece of galangal, peeled and finely chopped

4–6 garlic cloves, peeled and finely chopped

4 Thai shallots or 2 regular shallots, peeled and finely chopped

1 tsp grated zest of kaffir lime

1 tbsp curry powder

1½ tsp ground turmeric

for the curry

2 tbsp vegetable oil

1 x 400-ml/14-fl oz can of coconut milk

200 ml/7 fl oz/scant 1 cup water

4 new potatoes or small potatoes, quartered

6 Thai shallots, peeled or 3 regular shallots, peeled and halved

400 g/14 oz skinned, boneless chicken thigh meat, cut into chunks

2–3 tbsp *nam pla* (fish sauce)

1–2 tsp palm sugar

a squeeze of lime juice

to garnish

a handful of Thai sweet basil

a scattering of Thai shallots, finely sliced and fried until crisp (optional)

2 dried red chillies, fried until crisp (optional)

To make the paste: toast the dried chillies in a dry pan over a low heat for a few minutes, being careful not to burn them. Set aside to cool, then use a pair of scissors to cut off the stems and slit them lengthways. Scrape out and discard the seeds. Cut the chillies up into small pieces and soak in warm water for 20 minutes or until soft.

In the same dry pan, toast the cardamom seeds, coriander seeds, cumin seeds and black peppercorns until fragrant. Set aside.

Using a pestle and mortar, start pounding and grinding the paste ingredients, beginning with the chillies and the salt, and then working from the hardest ingredients on to the softest (in the order listed), making sure each ingredient is well incorporated before adding the next. You should end up with a homogenized paste – try to get it as smooth as possible, but don't worry too much. You can do this in a blender, but you may need to add between 1–2 tablespoons of water to keep the paste from gumming up the blades, while making sure it does not become too loose.

To make the curry: heat the oil in a saucepan or wok over a medium heat, and then fry the paste until you can really smell all the spices, about 30–40 seconds. Add the coconut milk, and bring it to the boil, blending in the paste. Then add 100 ml/3½ fl oz/scant ½ cup of the water and stir it together. Add the potatoes and shallots, and bring back to the boil. Add the chicken and bring back to the boil again. If the sauce looks a little thick, add the remaining water.

Simmer gently for about 5–10 minutes, or until chicken, shallots and potatoes are cooked. Add the *nam pla*, sugar and squeeze of lime. Taste and adjust the seasoning.

Garnish with the handful of Thai basil at the last minute, the deep-fried shallots and the dried red chillies, if using. Serve accompanied with rice.

Variations

As with most curries, you can replace the main protein with pretty much anything you like. One of my favourite versions of this is called *gaeng kari pla salmon fukthong*, with salmon and pumpkin.

To make it, add 100 g/3½ oz peeled pumpkin, cut into 2-cm/¾-inch chunks, when you would have added the chicken and potatoes. Simmer for 10 minutes, until the pumpkin is cooked, add the lime juice and *nam pla*, to taste, and then add 200 g/7 oz skinned salmon, also cut into 2-cm/¾-inch chunks. It should take just 2 more minutes to cook the salmon. Remove from the heat, add a handful of Thai sweet basil leaves, and serve.

To make this completely vegan, add 250 g/9 oz peeled pumpkin and 150 g/5 oz peeled green papaya where you would add the chicken and potatoes. Simmer until the vegetables are cooked, about 10–15 minutes. Then season with lime juice and light soy sauce, to taste. Finally, remove from the heat and add the sweet basil.

~ *When using fresh turmeric, you may want to wear disposable gloves. It STAINS. (Don't use your favourite chopping board, either.)* ~

~ *If you want to use store-bought paste, I recommend Nittaya or Mae Ploy brands of yellow curry paste for this recipe. Use 2 heaped tablespoons in place of the home-made paste, and then follow the recipe as normal.* ~

~ *Each batch of paste – whether home-made or store-bought – will taste slightly different depending on its age and the strength of components, so always TASTE to avoid surprises!* ~

Gaeng Massaman

Massaman Curry

This is probably the most complex of the Thai curries to make. And, while there are acceptable *massaman* pastes available to buy in the shops, it's worth the effort to make from scratch because all the subtle fragrances of the freshly ground spices vanish if the paste sits around for too long.

Its complexity stems from the fact that the dish is not initially Thai. It either came to Thailand with spice traders in the Muslim south of the country, or (and this is my preferred story) it arrived at the Court of Siam with the first Persian envoys in the seventeenth century.

Most commonly, you'll find it made with beef or chicken. I find it works beautifully with goat, and so I've used it here.

Photographed on page 72, bottom left.

Serves 4–6

for the paste

4 Thai shallots or 2 regular shallots

4 garlic cloves

1 coriander (cilantro) root (see page 203)

12 long dried chillies

1 cinnamon stick

1 tbsp cumin seeds

1 tbsp coriander seeds

a pinch of sea salt

2 cloves

seeds of 1 cardamom pod

¼ tsp black peppercorns

2 sticks lemongrass, bashed and finely chopped

¼ nutmeg, grated

1 heaped tbsp *kapi* (shrimp paste)

for the curry

2 tbsp ghee

400 g/14 oz goat, cubed

2 tbsp vegetable oil

[*continues opposite, top*]

To make the paste: preheat the oven to 180°C fan/200°C/400°F/gas mark 6.

Wrap the shallots, garlic and coriander root tightly in aluminium foil and bake in the oven for about 20 minutes, or until soft.

Meanwhile, in a dry frying pan (skillet), toast the dried chillies until they are crispy, shaking them in the pan to ensure they don't burn. Set aside to cool, then snip them up into small pieces with scissors, discarding the stalks and the seeds. Soak the pieces in warm water for at least 20 minutes. Then dry them thoroughly with paper towels.

Toast the cinnamon stick, cumin seeds and coriander seeds in the dry pan until they're fragrant. Then grind the paste, starting with the dried chillies and the salt, followed by the toasted spices, the remaining dry spices, and the lemongrass. Peel the shallots and garlic, cut the coriander root into small pieces, and pound them into the paste, followed by the grated nutmeg and the *kapi*. Keep grinding until the paste is as smooth as possible, and everything is thoroughly incorporated.

Method continues opposite, top.

4 Thai shallots, peeled or 2 regular
  shallots, peeled and halved

4 new potatoes, halved

2 tbsp coconut cream

1 x 400-ml/14-fl oz can of coconut milk

a handful of raisins (optional)

200 ml/7 fl oz/scant 1 cup water

2 tbsp tamarind paste (purée)

6 cardamom pods, broken open

1 tbsp palm sugar

1–2 tbsp nam pla (fish sauce)

1–2 tbsp roasted peanuts

To make the curry: melt the ghee in a large frying pan, and gently brown the meat. You will need to do this in batches.

Heat the vegetable oil in a large wok or saucepan, then add the paste, and fry until it's very fragrant. Add the meat, shallots, potatoes and the coconut cream, and stir them thoroughly into the paste. Then add the coconut milk, raisins (if using) and water, bring up to the boil, and simmer for 30 minutes.

Now add the tamarind paste, cardamom, palm sugar and nam pla and gently simmer, partially covered, for another 30–40 minutes, until the meat is tender. About 10 minutes before you finish cooking, add the peanuts.

Finally, taste the curry and adjust the seasoning. You're looking for a sour start to its taste, which then develops in the mouth to become sweet and savoury.

Roti

Thai roti breads are akin to Indian paratha or Malaysian canai, and come from the Muslim south of the country. They can be served as a savoury accompaniment to curries, such as Gaeng Massaman (above) or the Gaeng Keow Wan made with beef (pages 63–65), or can be eaten smothered in butter and with condensed milk as a sweet treat.

Photographed on page 73, bottom right.

Makes 12

1 egg

4 tbsp milk

125 ml/4 fl oz/½ cup water

juice of ½ lime

½ tsp salt

1 tbsp caster (superfine) sugar

40 g/1½ oz/3 tbsp butter, melted

500 g/1 lb 2 oz plain (all-purpose)
  flour, sifted

125 ml/4 fl oz/½ cup vegetable oil, for
  coating and frying

In a large bowl, beat the egg with the milk and water until well combined. Add the lime juice and mix well. Add the salt and the sugar, then add the melted butter. Add the flour gradually, mixing as you go – you may not need all of it. When it is thick enough to handle, mix with your hands until it comes together to form a dough. Using any leftover flour to sprinkle over a cool work surface, knead the dough for about 5–8 minutes until you have a smooth ball.

Divide the dough into 12 pieces. Roll each piece into a ball. Coat each ball with oil, place in a bowl and leave to rest, covered with a damp dish towel, for 2 hours.

When the resting period is up, use a rolling pin to roll out each piece of dough into a square as thin as you can. Taking the dough by a corner, carefully twist each piece into a rope and then coil each rope into a snail-shaped roll. Flatten each one with the palm of your hand and roll out again into discs about 16–18 cm/6–7 inches in diameter.

Heat a smallish frying pan (skillet) and add a little oil. When hot, gently fry each roti, one at a time, on both sides until golden brown. You may need to replenish the oil as you go. Remove and serve warm. Before eating, slap the roti from hand to hand to make it extra flaky.

Kua Kling Kwang

Southern Dry Venison Curry

This is one of southern Thailand's most famous curries. It is fragrant, a little salty and fiercely hot. And, despite its fame, it is unusual among the Thai curries for its dryness. There is no oil used in its cooking, and it has no sauce.

This recipe makes a large portion, but if you have leftovers, you can use them in a Thai omelette or serve them in lettuce cups as you would *laarp*.

Photographed on page 72, top left.

Serves 4–6

for the paste

15 dried red bird's eye (bird) chillies (see tip)

10–12 fresh red Thai bird's eye chillies, coarsely chopped

a good pinch of salt

1 tbsp black peppercorns

3 sticks lemongrass, bashed and chopped

2 tbsp chopped galangal

6 large coriander (cilantro) roots (see page 203), chopped (or substitute 1 heaped tbsp of chopped stems)

4 tbsp chopped fresh turmeric

zest of 1 small kaffir lime

4 small garlic cloves

2 Thai shallots or 1 regular shallot, sliced

1 tbsp *kapi* (shrimp paste)

for the curry

200 g/7 oz minced (ground) pork

300 g/10½ oz minced (ground) venison

1 tsp palm sugar

1–2 tbsp *nam pla* (fish sauce)

1 tsp ground turmeric (optional)

6 kaffir lime leaves, finely sliced

1 stick lemongrass, finely sliced

To make the paste: toast the dried chillies in a hot, dry frying pan (skillet) for a few moments until they are very crispy, shaking them constantly to keep them from burning. Using scissors, snip off the stem ends, then snip them up into small pieces, removing the seeds as you go. Soak the pieces in warm water for about 20 minutes. Drain and dry on paper towels.

Then, with a pestle and mortar, pound the paste ingredients together in the order listed above (alternatively, blitz them together in a blender along with 1–2 tbsp of water) until you have a smooth-ish paste.

To make the curry: heat a wok over a medium heat until it's good and hot. Add the paste and start stirring and scraping until it's really fragrant, no more than 1 minute. Note that this curry does not use any oil, so it's important to keep the paste moving to ensure it doesn't burn. If it looks like it is sticking too much, add a dash of water.

Now add the pork to bring some fat and moisture to the paste, turning and cooking and mixing it through the flavours. Then add the venison, really scraping and stir-frying it through the paste and pork. You want everything well combined and cooked through. Add the palm sugar and 1 tbsp of *nam pla*, stirring through. Add the ground turmeric, if using. Taste and add more *nam pla* if needed – the curry should be very hot, fragrant and salty.

Remove from the heat and stir through the lime leaves and the lemongrass. Serve with freshly cooked rice and some crunchy vegetables on the side.

~ *If you can't find dried Thai bird's eye chillies, African dried peri peri chilies make a good substitution.* ~

Gaeng Leung Pla Kup Saparot

Southern Spicy Sour Curry
with Fish and Pineapple

Khun Tieb Watjanakaomkul, our friends Lek and Yai's mum, is a remarkable 77 year old woman and a legendary cook. Her parents were rice farmers, but she insisted on studying instead of working in the paddy fields, a revolutionary act back then, when Thai society in general, let alone rural areas, did not think a woman's education was important. Secondly, she convinced her mother to let her move away to Hat Yai, where she met her husband, who was Thai-Chinese. Cross-cultural marriages used to be most unusual. She made it work. She cooks both Thai and Chinese food brilliantly, and this is her recipe.

In the south, they call this soupy curry *gaeng som*. We call it *gaeng leung* to differentiate it from the *gaeng som* of central Thailand. '*Som*' means 'sour', and both curries are. Yet, this is a very different beast: it's packed with turmeric and chillies and soured with lime juice, rather than the tamarind of the plains.

I use a blender for this paste – but beware: it will turn yellow. As will your hands if you don't wear gloves.

Photographed on page 73, top right.

Serves 4–6

10–12 Thai bird's eye chillies

12–15-cm/5–6-inch piece of fresh turmeric, scraped and chopped

4 garlic cloves, peeled and chopped

2 Thai shallots or 1 regular shallot, peeled and chopped

a pinch of salt

1 tbsp *kapi* (shrimp paste)

½ ripe pineapple, peeled, cored and thinly sliced

300 g/10½ oz firm white fish fillet, sliced

4–6 tbsp lime juice

salt or *nam pla* (fish sauce), to taste

Place the chillies, turmeric, garlic, shallots and salt together into a mini chopper or blender with 100 ml/3½ fl oz/scant ½ cup of water. Blitz to a smooth paste.

In a large saucepan, add the turmeric mixture to 600 ml/1 pint/2½ cups of water. Bring to the boil, then add the *kapi*. Do not stir, as the soup will turn cloudy. Add the pineapple and bring back to the boil. Add the fish and bring up to the boil until the fish is just cooked. Remove from the heat and add half of the lime juice. Taste, and add more if needed, plus the salt or *nam pla* – you might need more than you think, so keep tasting: it should be sour and hot with the sweetness of the pineapple coming through. Serve with rice and the *Moo Khem* (Salty Pork, page 122).

Gaeng Panang

Panang Curry

This dry curry most likely has its roots in Malaysia, or maybe even further west. It first appears in Thai cookbooks in the late nineteenth century, and reflects the aristocratic style of cooking from that period, when many spices were too expensive for ordinary Thais. It is rich, thick, salty and sweet, with the peanuts in the paste making this unique in the Thai canon. Alas, if you have an issue with peanuts, this is not for you – they're non-negotiable.

The nineteenth century versions of the recipe call for beef, but you can also make this with chicken. Those older versions would also do away with the garnishes, and with the clove of garlic used here to flavour the oil before cooking off the paste.

Serves 4–6

for the paste

10 long dried red chillies

1 tsp cumin seeds

1 tsp coriander seeds

a pinch of salt

2 sticks lemongrass, finely chopped

2.5-cm/1-inch piece of galangal, peeled and finely chopped

2 tbsp peanuts, toasted (see tip)

3 coriander (cilantro) roots (see page 203), finely chopped

4 Thai shallots or 2 regular shallots, peeled and chopped

4 garlic cloves, peeled and chopped

zest of 1 kaffir lime

1 tsp *kapi* (shrimp paste)

for the curry

3 tbsp vegetable oil

1 garlic clove, finely chopped

300 g/10½ oz beef or chicken thighs, cut into strips

2 tbsp *nam pla* (fish sauce)

1 tbsp palm sugar

175 ml/6 fl oz/¾ cup coconut cream

1 long red chilli, deseeded, finely sliced

3 kaffir lime leaves, finely sliced

a handful of holy basil leaves, to finish

First make the paste: in a dry frying pan (skillet), toast the dried chillies for a few minutes until they're crispy and brittle. Keep them moving in the pan as you go to make sure they don't burn. Let cool a little, then cut the stalks off the chillies with scissors, and snip them into very small pieces, removing the seeds as you go. Soak in warm water for about 20 minutes, then drain and dry thoroughly on paper towels.

In the same dry pan, toast the cumin and coriander seeds for 1–2 minutes, until fragrant. Remove from the heat and transfer to a mortar and pestle. Add the salt, and grind the seeds. Now add the chillies, and pound until broken down and smooth. Then work through the remaining paste ingredients in the order listed until you have a smooth paste. If you prefer, you can blitz everything together in a food processor. To do so, you will need to add 1–2 tbsp of water to help the paste come together. Add everything in the same order, as above.

To make the curry: heat the oil in a wok or saucepan, and fry off the garlic until golden. Then add the curry paste and fry for about 1 minute, until fragrant. Now add the meat, stirring it through the paste thoroughly. Keep it moving in the pan for a couple of minutes, then add the *nam pla* and sugar. Stir to combine, then add the coconut cream. Work it thoroughly through the paste, then simmer gently, without stirring, until the meat is cooked, about 3–4 minutes. Remove from the heat, then stir the chilli and lime leaves through the curry, followed by the basil.

~ *The type of peanuts I prefer to use are often sold as pink peanuts. They still have their pinkish skins on and they're unsalted. Toast them in a dry pan until they become a little crisp and have char marks. Let them cool before peeling, then the skins will just slip off.* ~

Gaeng Pah

Jungle Curry

As the name suggests, this curry has its origins in... you guessed it... the jungle, and from a time when folks living in the forested parts of Thailand had to make do and mend. This means, for a start, that there's no coconut milk in it. And like *Gaeng Ohm* (Northeastern Pork and Vegetable Curry, page 81), it is a dish whose roots lie in foraged ingredients. Traditionally, it would have been made with wild boar, and since that's now readily available, I have chosen to use it here. But you can make it with any protein you like. One of the best versions I ever had, at Pailin in Los Angeles's Thai Town, was made with slices of catfish. I've also had it made with rabbit, quail and with water beetles. The choice is yours.

Serves 4–6

for the paste

10 dried bird's eye (bird) chillies

5 dried long red chillies

a good pinch of salt

2.5-cm/1-inch piece of galangal, finely chopped

2 lemongrass sticks, finely sliced

2–4 red Thai bird's eye chillies

1 Thai shallot or ½ regular shallot, peeled and finely chopped

2 tbsp chopped *krachai* (fingerroot/ Chinese keys, see page 203)

3 garlic cloves, peeled and finely chopped

zest of 1 kaffir lime

1½ tsp *kapi* (shrimp paste)

for the curry

1 tbsp vegetable oil

300 g/10½ oz wild boar or pork, cut into 2-cm/¾-inch strips

2 tbsp *nam pla* (fish sauce)

4–6 round Thai aubergines (eggplants), quartered

2.5-cm/1-inch piece of *krachai* (finger-root/Chinese keys), finely sliced

2–3 strands of fresh green peppercorns

3–4 kaffir lime leaves, torn

a small handful of holy basil leaves

To make the paste: toast the dried chillies in a dry frying pan (skillet) until brittle. Keep them moving in the pan to keep them from burning. Then, soak them in hot water for 10 minutes. Drain and dry them thoroughly. Cut them into very small pieces with scissors, removing the seeds as you go. You may want to use gloves for this so that you don't burn your hands on the capsaicin.

In a pestle and mortar, pound the dried chillies together with the salt to break them down. Then work through the remaining paste ingredients in the order listed, pounding them together until you have a smooth paste.

To make the curry: heat the vegetable oil in a saucepan, and fry off the paste until it's fragrant. Add the meat and stir it quickly through the paste. Add the *nam pla* and 700 ml/1¼ pints/scant 3 cups water, stir everything gently together and bring to a gentle boil. Add the aubergines, *krachai* and the lime leaves, and cook for about 5 minutes, until the pork or boar is done. Remove from the heat, stir in the basil leaves, and serve.

Bpu Pat Pong Kari Chao Lay

Curried Crab from Chao Lay Restaurant

Khun Thip paused when she gave me this recipe. Then she said, 'Why don't you move here to Hua Hin. Then we can teach you all our recipes, and we can open a cooking school for *farang*.' I was very tempted, not least because Chao Lay is one of my favourite places to eat in the world, and this is my favourite of their dishes. It is rich, creamy, spicy and delicious.

You can order it two ways. In the first, the crab comes in its shell, so there's a lot of claw cracking and finger licking. The second way is made with lump crab only, in which case replace the whole crab below with 400 g/14 oz of it. Do take care when you're cooking not to break it up; part of the dish's joy lies in the sweet crab meat's contrast with the sauce.

Serves 2–4

4–6 tbsp vegetable oil

8 garlic cloves, peeled and chopped

1 onion, sliced lengthways

3 tbsp hot curry powder

2 swimmer crabs, cooked, cleaned and cut into 4

120 g/4 oz lump crab meat

1 x 400-ml/14-fl oz can of evaporated milk

2 tbsp *nam pla* (fish sauce)

1 tbsp caster (superfine) sugar

a good grinding of white pepper

1 tbsp chilli oil

3 eggs, lightly beaten

a small handful of Chinese celery leaves

a small handful of spring onions (scallions), cut into 2-cm/ ¾-inch batons

2 Thai long red chillies, deseeded and finely sliced

Heat the wok over a high heat and, when it's hot, add the vegetable oil. When the oil starts to shimmer, add the garlic and onion, and stir-fry until fragrant without letting it colour. Add the curry powder, stir it through, then add the crab. Stir gently but thoroughly to coat the crab in the curry powder, oil and onion. Then add the evaporated milk and bring to a simmer. Add the *nam pla*, sugar and white pepper, and stir together.

In a small bowl, add the chilli oil to the eggs, and beat gently with a fork until combined. Pour the mixture into the simmering curry and, when it starts to thicken, stir it through the sauce. Finally, add the celery leaves, spring onions and chillies, stirring everything together. Remove from the heat and serve with rice.

Gaeng Hang Lay

Pork Curry with Pickled Garlic and Ginger

This pork curry from Northern Thailand has its roots in Myanmar. I am always astounded by its complexity and depth. It is not an especially fiery curry; instead it has a rich, sweet, salty sourness punctuated by fresh ginger and tart pickled garlic. I use two cuts of pork because the belly adds fattiness and the shoulder gives texture. Typically, this would be made with a *hang lay* powder, but it can be hard to find, so I use a Thai curry powder or a good Madras.

Serves 4–6

for the paste

12 long dried red chillies

a pinch of sea salt

2-cm/¾-inch piece of galangal, peeled and chopped

1 stick lemongrass, chopped

4 garlic cloves, chopped

2 Thai shallots or 1 regular shallot, peeled and chopped

1 tsp *kapi* (shrimp paste)

for the curry

250 g/9 oz pork belly, chunked

250 g/9 oz pork shoulder (butt), chunked

3 tbsp Thai or Madras curry powder

2 tbsp *nam kratiem dong* (the liquid from a jar of pickled garlic)

2 tbsp vegetable oil

300 ml/10 fl oz/1¼ cups stock

7-cm/2¾-inch piece of ginger, peeled and finely slivered

6 Thai shallots, peeled and halved or 3 regular shallots, peeled and quartered

1–2 teaspoons light soy sauce, to taste

1 tbsp dark soy sauce

1–2 tsp *nam pla* (fish sauce), to taste

1 tbsp palm sugar

100 ml/3½ fl oz/½ cup coconut milk

3–4 tbsp tamarind paste (purée), to taste

a good pinch of ground turmeric

4–6 heads of pickled garlic, peeled and cloves separated (chopped if large)

100 g/3½ oz unsalted peanuts, roasted

To make the paste: in a dry frying pan (skillet), lightly toast the dried chillies until fragrant, no more than 30 seconds. Fill a bowl with boiling water, and soak the chillies for 20 minutes, or until softened. Drain and dry them well on paper towels. Cut into small pieces with scissors.

In a pestle and mortar, pound the paste ingredients together in the order listed, making sure each one is well incorporated before moving on to the next. You can use a mini-chopper for this if you prefer, but you will need to add about 1–2 tbsp of water to keep the blade happy.

To make the curry: in a large bowl, mix the two cuts of pork together with the Thai curry powder, 1 tbsp of the pickled garlic juice and the curry paste, and place in the refrigerator to marinate for at least 1 hour, ideally up to 3 hours.

Heat the oil in a wok and stir-fry the pork until it has lost its pinky colour, about 10–15 minutes or so. Add the stock, bring up to the boil, then simmer over a low heat for about 25 minutes.

Add the ginger and shallots, and cook over a low heat, partially covered, for 30 minutes.

Finally, add the light soy sauce, dark soy sauce, *nam pla*, sugar, coconut milk, tamarind, a good pinch of ground turmeric, the remaining pickled garlic juice, the pickled garlic and the peanuts, and simmer gently, uncovered, for another 30–40 minutes. Add a splash of water if ever it looks a little dry. Taste and adjust the seasoning – it should be rich, sweet and salty, and the pork should be tender.

Serve with rice.

~ Thai pickled garlic heads are generally smaller than Chinese, so if using Chinese, just use 2–3. ~

Gaeng Ohm

Northeastern Pork and Vegetable Curry

Packed with vegetables, dill and chillies, this deliciously pungent curry is typical of northeastern Thailand, and – forget whiskers on kittens – it's one of my favourite things. The pungency comes from *pla ra*, which is impossible to translate directly, but is basically fermented fish. Think of an extra-funky, thick, unfiltered fish sauce, and you're halfway there.

Serves 4–6

for the paste

4 sticks lemongrass

1 kaffir lime leaf, finely sliced

6–8 red chillies

6 garlic cloves

4–6 Thai shallots, or 2 regular shallots, chopped

6–8 tbsp *pla ra* (Isaan fermented fish sauce)

for the curry

300 g/10½ oz pork loin, sliced

2 tbsp vegetable oil

600 ml/1 pint/2½ cups water or stock

6 Thai aubergines (eggplants), quartered, plus a handful of pea aubergines (eggplants), about 30 g/1 oz in all

300 g/10½ oz pumpkin, peeled and diced

100 g/3½ oz bamboo shoots, shredded

a large handful of Thai sweet basil

5 kaffir lime leaves

a large bunch of dill, cut into 5-cm/2-inch pieces

a dash of *nam pla* (fish sauce)

To make the paste: remove the outer sheath from the lemongrass and give it a good bash. Chop it up small, then smash in a mortar and pestle. Add the thinly sliced lime leaf and the chillies and bash again. Add the garlic and shallots and bash. Alternatively, do all of this in a chopper, adding a little water if needed.

Add the *pla ra* to the paste and then work it into the pork slices. Marinate for 1 hour in the refrigerator.

To make the curry: heat the oil in a large saucepan and fry the meat and paste until cooked and fragrant, about 3–4 minutes. Add the water or stock and bring up to a simmer. Add the vegetables and cook until they're just done, about 2–3 minutes. Finally, add the herbs and a dash more water, if necessary. Add *nam pla* to taste, and a little more *pla ra* if you like. We want this to be hot, salty and a bit funky! Serve with rice.

Gaeng Som Goong Kai Jeow Cha Om

Sour Curry with Prawns served with a Tropical Acacia-leaf Omelette

This is a real central Thailand dish from the ancient capital of Sukhothai. It is sour, pungent and spicy, and shot through with the area's big ingredient: tamarind.

It also contains an omelette made with *cha om*, or tropical acacia leaf – it looks like a fern and, though it smells a bit like chicken poop, is delicious once cooked. Beware though: the stems have very sharp thorns. Carefully denude them of the lush leaves, and discard the rest. If you cannot find *cha om*, don't worry: you can use chives or spring onions (scallions) instead.

Serves 4–6

for the curry paste
6 long dried chillies
a pinch of salt
1 tbsp chopped galangal
4 Thai shallots or 2 regular shallots, peeled and chopped
2 tsp *kapi* (shrimp paste)

for the omelette
4 eggs
a dash of *nam pla* (fish sauce)
a good grinding of white pepper
200 g/7 oz *cha om* (acacia leaf), leaves only (if unavailable, substitute chives or spring onions/scallions)
vegetable oil, for frying

for the curry
200 g/7 oz raw prawns (shrimp), peeled and de-veined but with the tails left on, 4 finely chopped
2 tbsp tamarind paste (purée)
1 tsp sugar
2 tbsp *nam pla* (fish sauce)
150 g/5½ oz daikon (mooli), halved lengthways and sliced
65 g/2¼ oz sliced bamboo shoots
6 cherry tomatoes
100 g/3½ oz *pak boong* (Siamese watercress), trimmed and chopped

To make the paste: toast the dried chillies in a hot, dry frying pan (skillet) for a few moments until they are very crispy, shaking them constantly to keep them from burning. Using scissors, snip off the stem ends, then snip them up into small pieces, removing the seeds as you go. Soak the pieces in warm water for about 20 minutes. Drain and dry on paper towels.

Pound all the ingredients for the paste together in a pestle and mortar until smooth. Set aside.

To make the omelette, in a large bowl, beat the eggs together with a splash of *nam pla* and some ground white pepper, then add the *cha om*.

In a deep frying pan (skillet), heat a 2.5-cm/1-inch depth of oil until VERY hot. Pour in the eggs and swirl to coat the pan. Fry until cooked and golden, flip, then remove from the oil with a slotted spoon and drain on paper towels. Let cool, then chop the omelette into squares and set aside.

To make the curry: bring 1 litre/1¾ pints/ 4 cups of water to the boil. Add the 4 chopped prawns and simmer until cooked. Remove the prawns from the water and work them gently into the paste in the pestle and mortar until combined.

Return the water to the boil, add the tamarind, sugar and *nam pla*, then add the paste and return to the boil. Add the daikon and bring back to the boil. Then add the bamboo shoots, tomatoes and *pak boong*, and return to the boil once again. Finally, add the whole prawns and simmer for a couple of minutes until cooked. Taste and adjust the seasoning: it should be sour, salty and spicy.

Serve in bowls, topped with the squares of omelette.

~ *Thai omelettes are drier than Western ones, so cook the egg thoroughly in hot oil.* ~

Gaeng Tup Gai Taang Tai

Southern Chicken Liver Curry

One of the things I love about this curry is the way it juxtaposes the creaminess of the chicken livers with the salty-spiciness of the sauce. It is one of my most requested dishes. In my humble opinion, we do not eat enough chicken livers. If you're someone who has in the past felt squeamish about them, this may just be the dish to change your mind.

Serves 4

for the paste

6–8 large dried chillies (depending on how hot you like it)

1 tsp cumin seeds

1 tsp coriander seeds

a pinch of sea salt

1 tsp black peppercorns

1 tbsp finely chopped galangal

2 sticks lemongrass, bashed, peeled and finely chopped

3 garlic cloves, peeled and finely chopped

2 tbsp finely chopped fresh turmeric (see tip)

1 heaped tsp *kapi* (shrimp paste)

for the curry

2 tbsp vegetable oil

250 ml/9 fl oz/generous 1 cup coconut milk mixed with 150 ml/5 fl oz/⅔ cup stock or water, or 1 x 400-ml/14-fl oz can of coconut milk

100 ml/3½ fl oz/scant ½ cup chicken stock

1 tbsp *nam kratiem dong* (the liquid from a jar of pickled garlic)

1 tbsp white vinegar

1 tbsp caster (superfine) sugar

2 tbsp *nam pla* (fish sauce)

a small handful of fresh green peppercorns

350 g/12 oz chicken livers, trimmed

a good handful of Thai sweet basil

deep-fried garlic (page 204), to garnish

To make the paste: toast the dried chillies in a hot, dry frying pan (skillet) for a few moments until they are very crispy, shaking them constantly to keep them from burning. Using scissors, snip off the stem ends, then snip them up into small pieces, removing the seeds as you go. Soak the pieces in warm water for about 20 minutes. Drain and dry on paper towels.

Toast the cumin seeds and the coriander seeds in the same dry pan over a low heat until just fragrant, about 1–2 minutes.

With a pestle and mortar, pound the paste ingredients together in the order listed (alternatively, blitz them together in a blender along with 1–2 tbsp of water) until you have a smooth-ish paste. If it is not as smooth as a commercial one, don't worry, it will still taste terrific.

To make the curry: heat the oil in a wok or heavy-based pan. Add the paste and stir-fry until really fragrant, just 2 minutes. Add the coconut milk and bring to the boil. Add the chicken stock, the *nam kratiem dong*, vinegar, sugar, *nam pla* and the green peppercorns. Bring back to the boil, then taste and adjust the seasoning if necessary. You're looking for a balance of sweet, hot, sour, salty and spicy.

You can make the curry up to this point and finish it later – or even the next day, if necessary.

If finishing it now, add the chicken livers and cook for a few minutes until just done.

If finishing it later, bring the curry sauce back to the boil, and cook the chicken livers in it as above.

Finally, stir in the basil and garnish with deep-fried garlic. Serve with rice.

~ Wear some disposable gloves when dealing with turmeric root, or you will have yellow-stained fingers! ~

Soups
and
Braises

เลี้ยงอาหารอย่างไม่มีพิธี
INFORMAL DINNER

WATER WINE

DESSERT SERVICE A

(11) dessert plate,
(13) finger bowl,
(15) dessert spoon,

TABLE SET WITH SOUP COURSE

1 — service plate   2 — soup with it's own plate   3 — dinner fork   4 — dinner knife   5 — salad
6 — soup spoons or cocktail fork   7 — dessert spoon and fork   8 — salt and pepper   9 — cigarettes   10 —

อาหารชุดแรกจะเสิร์ฟโดยผู้รับใช้ หลัง
จากแขกนั่งลงเรียบร้อยแล้วและหยิบผ้าเช็ดมือ
...อาหาร หรือชามซุป ชุดแรกจัด
...ถ้าคนรับใช้เสิร์ฟ
...นั่งเรียบร้อยแล้ว
...อาหาร หรือครัว
...ย่างแรก ในมือซ้าย
...เริ่มต้นด้วยสุภาพ
...าพชาย และจบด้วย
...ทานอาหารชุดแรกเสร็จ
...ซุป และเก็บจานจากทาง
...จากได้ แล้ววางจานใหม่
...เสิร์ฟต่อไป แล้วคนรับใช้

จะทำงานอาหารชุดใหญ่วางมาบนมือข้า...
ทางด้านซ้ายเสิร์ฟให้แขกทุกคน รวมทั้ง...
ควรถือในระดับ ที่แขกจะหยิบอาหาร ได้สะ...
แล้วจึงนำซามอาหารผักมาทั้งสองมือ (ชาม...
ผักสองชาม) โดยใช้ผ้าเช็ดมือพับรองมือ...
กันร้อน ส่งชามในมือซ้ายก่อน แล้วจึงลง...
ในมือขวา ชามผักทั้งสองนี้ควรวางลงแน...
สำหรับตักกว่าจะควาลง ให้ตามแน่นปรก...
เพื่อจับได้สะดวก นำซ้อสหรือน้ำราดซ...
เสิร์ฟติด ๆ กันกับอาหารที่ต้องใช้ช้อสราด ...
จำไว้ว่า อาหารร้อนนั้นร้อนจริงและ...
เย็นก็ควรเย็นเต็มที่

ระหว่างที่รับประทานอาหารชุดใหญ่ ...
รับใช้ควรเติมน้ำตามถ้วยเมื่อจวนจะหมด แ...
ถ้าเสิร์ฟเหล้าต้องหมั่นคอยเติมแก้วเหล้า

เมื่ออาหารชุดให...
ซึ่งเป็นเวลาที่ไม่ควร มี...
แขกเลย จบอาหารชุด...
ออกก่อน แล้วจึงเอ...
หมด นอกจากคอกไ...
หรือที่เขี่ยบุหรี่ หีบบุ...
ประทานของหวาน เช...
ของชาวยุโรป) แก้...
เสิร์ฟเหล้าขณะรับประท...
นั่งควรใช้ผ้าเช็ดมือพับ...
หรือถาด

(2)

Three Basic Stocks

Thai Chicken Stock

Makes 2 litres/4 pints

1.5 kg/3 lb 5 oz chicken or chicken wings

1 small onion, peeled and halved or 4 spring onions (scallions)

1 garlic bulb, halved

6–8 coriander (cilantro) roots (see page 203), lightly bruised

½ large daikon (mooli), about 300 g/ 10½ oz, peeled and thickly sliced

1 tsp white peppercorns

Put everything in a stock pot with 3 litres/6 pints/12½ cups water to cover, and bring JUST to the boil. Then turn down the heat, and simmer *very* gently for about 2–2½ hours. Strain through a muslin-(cheesecloth-) lined sieve (strainer). Leave to cool, and skim any fat from the top before using.

Thai Pork Stock

Makes 2 litres/4 pints

1 kg/2 lb 4 oz assorted pork bones or pork ribs

1 onion, peeled and halved or 4 spring onions (scallions)

1 garlic bulb, halved

6–8 coriander (cilantro) roots (see page 203), lightly bruised

½ large daikon (mooli), about 300 g/ 10½ oz, peeled and thickly sliced

1 tsp white peppercorns

6–8 baby sweetcorn, halved

2–3 celery stalks, with leaves

2.5-cm/1-inch piece of fresh ginger, peeled (optional)

Put everything into the stock pot with 3 litres/6 pints/12½ cups water to cover, and then proceed exactly as per the method above.

Thai Vegetable Stock

Makes 2 litres/4 pints

1 onion, peeled and halved or 4 spring onions (scallions)

1 garlic bulb, halved

6–8 coriander (cilantro) roots (see page 203), lightly bruised

½ large daikon (mooli), about 300 g/ 10½ oz, peeled and thickly sliced

1 tsp white peppercorns

6–8 baby sweetcorn, halved

2–3 celery stalks, with leaves

2.5-cm/1-inch piece of fresh ginger, peeled (optional)

Put everything in the stock pot with 2 litres/ 4 pints/8¼ cups water to cover and proceed as above, but simmering for just 45 minutes.

On Thai Soups

The main purpose of Thai soups is to restore the palate. Or to kick it up a gear. *Gaeng cheud*, for example, literally means 'bland liquid', which doesn't sound all that exciting until you put it in context, as a palate cleanser of which you might have a spoon or two to reset yourself. It is supposed to be subtle. It is there to remind you that Thai food is not about HOT HOT HOT, but about balance, with spice, fragrance, neutrality and umami-ness dancing together around the glory of the rice.

But not all soups perform this neutral function: *Tom yum*, one of Thailand's most famous dishes, is hot and sour; sometimes very hot. *Tom kha* is rich with soothing coconut – holding the tension, like a good curry, between that richness and the fire of its chillies.

In choosing a soup to serve, you are not choosing a dish to appear alone before everything else, but a complement to dip into with your spoon as needed, and one that brings balance to the table.

On Vegetarian and Vegan Thai Food

It may come as a surprise, but there is no tradition of vegetarianism, let alone veganism, in Thai cooking. Certainly, plenty of Thais eat meat-free meals, but in most cases, they're leaving out the meat or fish while still using *nam pla* (fish sauce) and *kapi* (shrimp paste) in the usual places. Which, incidentally, is what a lot of restaurants used to do for vegetarian orders, too.

Over the last 30 years or so, however, a new Thai vegetarian cuisine has emerged. Some of the recipes in this book are vegetarian; some are vegan. And I have endeavoured to point them out when they crop up. Others, particularly the stir-fries, can be turned vegetarian by replacing the *nam pla* (fish sauce) with a light soy sauce. But the definitive book on the topic remains Vatcharin Bhumichitr's *Thai Vegetarian Cooking* from 1991. Alas, it is out of print at the time of writing, but it remains, as they say, the bomb…

Gaeng Cheud Mara

Stuffed Bitter Melon Soup

The word *cheud* is hard to translate: it sort of means 'flavourless', but in this case it means a simple, subtle, soothing backdrop to other spicy or rich dishes – something to balance out the meal.

Generally, this is served in a large pot on the table with some small bowls on the side. Take a spoonful between mouthfuls of fierier fare, or simply spoon it on to your rice.

If you can't find bitter melons (bitter gourds), you can easily replace them with cucumbers. Just peel the cucumbers, and add the peelings to the broth to add a hint of bitterness – but remember to remove them before serving! Alternatively, you could leave the melon out completely – just form the pork into mini meatballs and poach them in the stock, adding a few soaked mung-bean thread noodles, if you like.

Serves 4–6

4 garlic cloves, peeled

1 tsp white peppercorns

2–3 coriander (cilantro) roots
(see page 203)

2.5-cm/1-inch piece of fresh ginger,
peeled and finely chopped

a pinch of salt

250 g/9 oz minced (ground) pork

1–2 tsp *nam pla* (fish sauce), plus extra for
seasoning

a pinch of caster (superfine) sugar

1 tsp light soy sauce, plus extra for
seasoning

½ bitter melon (bitter gourd), cored and
cut into 6–8 fat slices

1.5 litres/2½ pints/6¼ cups chicken stock

spring onions (scallions), sliced,
to garnish

coriander (cilantro) leaves, sliced,
to garnish

Pound the garlic, peppercorns, coriander roots and ginger in a pestle and mortar with a little salt until you get a paste.

In a large bowl, mix the paste together with the pork, *nam pla*, sugar and soy sauce. Carefully stuff each fat slice of bitter melon with the pork mixture, and set aside.

In a large saucepan, bring the stock to the boil. Add splash of soy sauce and a splash of *nam pla*. Gently lower the stuffed melon slices into the soup stock. Cover and gently poach until cooked, about 10–15 minutes. Taste the stock and add more soy or *nam pla*, if desired.

Remove the stuffed melon slices to a serving bowl. Pour broth over the top and serve topped with spring onions and coriander leaves.

~ *To reduce the bitterness of the melon, you can simply blanch it whole in boiling water for about 1 minute. Drain and let cool before slicing and stuffing.* ~

Po Taek Talay

Spicy Seafood Soup

This recipe is not a million miles away from its famous cousin *Tom Yum* (Spicy and Sour Prawn Soup, page 90). The main differences are a lack of roasted chilli paste and that it involves more seafood. It combines an intense herby fragrance with a pure, subtle flavour. And it's incredibly easy to make.

Serves 4

1 litre/1¾ pints/4 cups water or stock

6-cm/2½-inch piece of galangal

2 sticks lemongrass, sliced diagonally

2 Thai shallots or 1 regular shallot, sliced

2 kaffir lime leaves

6–8 Thai bird's eye chillies, lightly bruised/crushed

100 g/3½ oz firm white fish, cut into pieces

100 g/3½ oz squid, cleaned and sliced into strips

8 large raw prawns (shrimp), peeled and de-veined but with the tails left on

12 mussels (see tip)

2 tbsp *nam pla* (fish sauce)

1–2 tbsp lime juice, to taste

a handful of Thai holy basil leaves

1–2 Thai bird's eye chillies, chopped (optional)

In a large heavy-based saucepan, bring the water or stock to the boil. Add the galangal, lemongrass, shallots, kaffir lime leaves and chillies, and bring back to the boil. Add the seafood, bring back to the boil, and simmer for a couple of minutes, until the seafood is cooked through. Don't stir, or the soup will go cloudy.

Remove the pan from the heat and add the fish sauce and lime juice. Taste and add more fish sauce or lime juice if needed – it should be sour, salty and spicy with a lovely herbal undertone.

Add the holy basil and the chopped bird's eyes, if using, and serve with *Nam Pla Prik* (Fish Sauce with Chillies, page 193) on the side.

~ Clean the mussels thoroughly under running water, pulling off any beards they may have. If any mussels are open, give them a firm tap with the back of a knife. If they refuse to close, discard them immediately. Any mussels that remain closed after cooking are dead, and should also be discarded. ~

Tom Yum Goong

Spicy and Sour Prawn Soup

Do I have to introduce this soup? Hot, sour and salty, with fat, sweet prawns – it is world famous, and justly so. It's also a doddle to make.

Well into retirement, Mum used to serve this soup quite formally as a starter at many a dinner party. That's not traditionally Thai at all, but it worked wonderfully because the soup is so light and it sharpens the appetite.

Serves 4-6

1 litre/1¾ pints/4 cups Thai Chicken Stock (page 86) or a stock made from the prawn heads and shells or water

6 thin slices of galangal

2 sticks lemongrass, bashed and sliced into 3–4 pieces

4 kaffir lime leaves, torn

4–6 Thai bird's eye chillies, lightly bruised

6 straw or oyster mushrooms, trimmed and halved

8–12 large prawns (shrimp) (about 400 g/14 oz), peeled and de-veined but with the tails left on (keep the heads and shells for stock, if wished)

3 tbsp *nam pla* (fish sauce), or to taste

1 tsp caster (superfine) sugar, or to taste

1½ tsp *nam prik pao* (roasted chilli paste, see page 203), or to taste

2 tbsp lime juice, or to taste

coriander (cilantro) leaves, to garnish

In a heavy-based saucepan, bring the stock or water to a boil over a medium heat. Add the sliced galangal, lemongrass, kaffir lime leaves and the chillies. Add the mushrooms and the prawns, then season with the fish sauce, sugar and *nam prik pao* to taste. Keep simmering until the prawns have turned a lovely coral colour and are cooked.

Remove from the heat and season with lime juice. Taste: you want it hot, sour, salty and spicy. Adjust to balance the four flavours. Serve in a large soup bowl garnished with the coriander leaves.

Tom Yum Gai

Spicy and Sour Chicken Soup

You can also make this soup with chicken (as photographed). Follow the recipe above to the point where you would add the mushrooms and the prawns, then add 350 g/12 oz sliced chicken breast and allow the broth to return to the boil. Add the *nam pla*, the *nam prik pao* and the sugar. Cook for 2–3 minutes, until the chicken is nearly done. Add the mushrooms, cook for another 2 minutes or so, so they retain some texture, then continue as above.

Tom Mamuang Pla

Fish and Green Mango Soup

Hailing from the coastal Chonburi region (home to the now notorious Pattaya Strip), this soup is simplicity itself. If you find yourself in the area, head to Na Klua market. It has hardly changed a dot since I was just a slip of a thing. Grab a beer, take a seat by the sea and order this soup from Platong Restaurant.

Serves 4–6

2 garlic cloves

4 green Thai bird's eye chillies

4 Thai shallots or 2 regular shallots, peeled and finely sliced

1 small green mango, cut into chunks

500 g/1 lb 2 oz firm white fish, cut into pieces

1–2 tbsp *nam pla* (fish sauce)

3–4 spring onions (scallions), trimmed and halved

a good pinch of salt

juice of 1 lime

a handful of Chinese celery leaves

In a large heavy-based saucepan, bring 1 litre/13/4 pints/4 cups of water to the boil.

Meanwhile, roughly crush the garlic and chillies in a mortar and pestle

When the water is boiling, add the crushed garlic and chilies and the shallots, and allow to simmer for a couple of minutes. Add the mango and simmer for a minute or so, then add the fish. Do not stir. Simmer for a few minutes and, when the fish is just cooked, add the *nam pla*, spring onions and salt. Remove from the heat and add the lime juice. Taste and adjust the seasoning. Add the Chinese celery and serve immediately.

Mother Water

If rice is the backbone of Thai food, then the rivers are its lifeblood. This is something reflected in the word for river itself – *mae nam*, literally 'mother water'. Without the river's waters, there can be no rice; thus, the river is the mother of it all.

The rains come and fill the paddies, which – in addition to the rice – give forth fish, crabs, snails and frogs. Free food. And the rains make the rivers run with life.

Recently, I visited the ancient capital of Sukhothai in what was still supposed to be the hot season. But the monsoon came early and hard, so hard that the River Yom had burst its banks. No one had seen it run like this in 20 years, but everyone was ready to take advantage of it. Wherever the water had dammed up against a road bridge or poured into the paddy fields, local men and women fished with giant nets strung on long bamboo poles. I have never seen so many fish caught at once, and every type you can imagine. I bought two big-head carp from them and persuaded the chef at our next stop to cook them for our dinner.

The Yom flows into the River Ping, which in turn joins the mighty Chao Praya, to create a spine of water that runs almost the length of the country to Bangkok; one that, in the evening light, looks like a vast dragon of beaten copper, slithering its way through the City of Angels to spew its fire into the sea.

The river – water – links everything together. To this day it provides vital transport links for both people and goods. The *khlongs* (canals) are not what they were when I was a girl – when Bangkok was still known as the Venice of the East. Most have been filled in. But back then, canals ran everywhere. I'd get in terrible trouble when I got caught wading or playing in the one on our street with my friends – because, you know, snakes. But you can still form a sense of what it was like if you take a longtail through the larger *khlongs*. Life comes right down to the water's edge. Kids play in it, people trade on it, and feed catfish outside waterside temples to make merit. (You may even see a snake or a monitor lizard on the banks, waiting for prey.)

And, of course, without the fish there can be no fish sauce – *nam pla*, literally 'fish water', which is as integral to Thai food as rice itself. Indeed, just as many Thais across the country continue to grow their own rice, so too do a very few ferment their own fish sauce at home in the traditional way.

As it says upon what must be one of the earliest Thai inscriptions, which dates from the late thirteenth century: *Nai nam mee pla, nai nah me kao* – 'In the time of King Ramkhamhaeng the Great, this land of Sukhothai is thriving. There is fish in the water and rice in the fields.'

Both are signs of plenty.

Kai Pa Lo

Pa Lo-style Braised Pork, Eggs and Kale

This is a very different style of Thai dish – a real Bangkok street favourite: sweet, salty, and somehow soothing with the scent of warm, fragrant, almost Middle-Eastern spices. It's a recipe that would have probably come into Thailand with Chinese immigrants in the early nineteenth century.

Traditionally, it would be made with a pork hock, but this version is easier for the home cook. I adapted it from a recipe given to me by Khun Tee, a steward I met on Thai Airways several years ago who, in turn, had got it from his grandmother. In food writing, I quickly learned, it always pays to carry pen and paper!

Serves 6

20 white peppercorns

3 coriander (cilantro) roots, coarsely chopped (see page 203)

4 small or 2 large garlic cloves, peeled and chopped

2 tbsp vegetable oil

500 g/1 lb 2 oz pork belly, cut into large pieces, or a combination of pork belly and pork ribs

1 tbsp five spice powder

4 tbsp sweet dark soy sauce

4 tbsp *nam pla* (fish sauce)

3 tbsp palm sugar

6–8 pieces of fried tofu (see tip), each about 4 cm/1½ inch square

12 hard-boiled quail's eggs (or 6 hen's eggs), peeled

a pinch of salt

a bunch of greens – chard, kale, pak choi (bok choy)

Pound the peppercorns, coriander roots and garlic together in a pestle and mortar to make a paste.

Pour 1.5 litres/3 pints/6¼ cups of water into a large stock pot and bring to the boil.

Meanwhile, heat the oil in a wok until hot, and stir-fry the paste. Add the pork and the five spice powder and continue to stir-fry until the meat has lost its pinkness, about 5–8 minutes.

Remove the pork from the oil and put it into the boiling water. Season with the soy sauce, *nam pla* and palm sugar, stir well, and simmer for 15 minutes. Add the tofu and simmer for 30 minutes, then add the eggs and simmer for another 15 minutes.

Taste. It should be sweet and salty, so adjust the seasoning at this point to suit your palate. Throw in the greens and let them wilt.

Serve with jasmine rice as a one-dish meal.

~ *You can easily buy fried tofu in most Asian food stores.* ~

Tom Kha Gai

Chicken and Coconut Soup

This soup, along with *Tom Yum* (page 90), is almost ubiquitous, and rightly so. Both are delicious, and, when well made, enter the top ten in the Thai food charts. The coconut milk softens some of the chilli's fire here, but it still packs a punch.

Serves 4–6 as part of a larger meal

250 ml/9 fl oz/generous 1 cup chicken stock

6-cm/2¼-inch piece of galangal, sliced into 4 or 5 pieces

2 sticks lemongrass, bashed, trimmed and roughly chopped

4 lime leaves, torn

400 g/14 oz skinless, boneless chicken thighs, cut into 1–2-cm/½–1-inch pieces

100 g/3½ oz oyster mushrooms

3–4 tbsp lime juice, to taste

3–4 tbsp *nam pla* (fish sauce), to taste

800 ml/1⅓ pints/3⅓ cups coconut milk

6 red Thai bird's eye chillies, lightly crushed

coriander (cilantro) leaves, to garnish

In a large heavy-based saucepan bring the stock, galangal, lemongrass and lime leaves to the boil. Add the chicken, mushrooms, 3 tbsp lime juice and 3 tbsp *nam pla*. Bring back to the boil until the chicken is cooked, just a couple of minutes. Add the coconut milk, stir it in well and bring back to the boil, then add the chillies. Taste for seasoning – you want it sour, creamy, salty and hot. Add more lime juice and *nam pla*, if you like.

Serve garnished with coriander leaves, with some *Nam Pla Prik* (Fish Sauce with Chillies, page 193) on the side.

Neua Tom Kem

Slow-braised Ox Cheek

My friend Mali Tiaree makes a version of this recipe with pork at the Puong Thong restaurant in Chiang Mai (for more on which, see page 164), which features in her daughter's excellent cookbook, *La Cuisine De Ma Mère*. People come from miles to eat it.

I like to make it with ox cheeks, which become meltingly tender when cooked so slowly. The resulting dish tastes surprisingly rich and complex, so much so, that it baffled Heston Blumenthal when I made it for him. (He was convinced that I'd used a sous vide. Not a chance!) It juxtaposes salt with sweet, and provides gentle hints of pepper, garlic and coriander at the end.

I like to serve a sharp vinegar sauce on the side to balance the sticky sweetness.

Serves 4–6

500 g/1 lb 2 oz ox cheeks, cut on the angle into 1–2-cm/½–1-inch slices

500 ml/17 fl oz/generous 2 cups stock or water

4 garlic cloves, peeled and chopped

4 coriander (cilantro) roots (see page 203), chopped

1 tbsp black peppercorns

2 tbsp palm sugar

6 tbsp *nam pla* (fish sauce)

2 tbsp dark soy sauce

1 tsp salt

1 tbsp vegetable oil

for the vinegar sauce (optional)

75 ml/2½ fl oz/⅓ cup white vinegar

1 tbsp caster (superfine) sugar

1 tbsp chopped large mild red chilli, deseeded

to garnish

1 large mild red chilli, finely sliced

a few sprigs of coriander (cilantro)

Put the ox cheek slices into a large saucepan or casserole with the stock or water, bring to the boil and simmer for about 15 minutes. Turn off the heat and let the beef sit in its bath for as long as it takes for the next steps.

In a pestle and mortar (or a blender) pound (or blend) the garlic, coriander roots and peppercorns into a paste – as smooth as you can. Set aside.

Mix the sugar, *nam pla*, soy sauce and salt together in a bowl.

Heat the oil in a wok or frying pan (skillet), add the garlic paste and sauté gently for 30 seconds, or until it's really fragrant. Be careful not to let the garlic burn. Add the paste into the bowl with the *nam pla* mixture and mix well.

Stir this mixture into the pan or casserole with the stock and beef, mixing well. Cover with a lid and simmer very gently over the lowest heat for 3 hours, until meltingly tender.

To make the vinegar sauce, combine the vinegar and sugar in a small saucepan and warm through until the sugar has dissolved. Cool and add the chopped red chilli.

Serve garnished with the finely sliced chilli and some sprigs of coriander.

Sup Hang Wua

Muslim Oxtail Soup

I knew I had to get a recipe from David Thompson. Lord knows, his big, pink book *Thai Food* – which most of us consider definitive – sits ragged and abused on my shelf, falling apart from use. It's a seminal tome.

David is also one of my Thai Food Heroes. More than anyone else, *farang* or Thai, he has researched, preserved, collated and revived many classic Thai recipes that might otherwise have been forgotten. Many of these he found in *nang sueh ngam sop*, memorial or funeral books, given out to mourners to commemorate the dead, and in this case often dating from the late nineteenth century. No one had ever thought to do it before, and it led to the Thai Government asking him to research the history of Thai cuisine.

The results of this research and his cooking are astounding. Some claim his Australian restaurant, Darley Street Thai, almost single-handedly launched a country-wide craze for Asian food. And his kitchens have spawned an army of brilliant chefs.

But what to ask for? It had to be something with ingredients that were easy to find... David suggested this soup. It's such a simple thing, but with simplicity comes a purity of flavour and a dash of technique. And this is one of my absolute favourite things. It is a little time consuming – just the beginning bit – but the reward is a sharp, slightly hot, spicy, herbal tangle of broth and tender meat.

Serves 6–8

for the oxtail

½ tsp salt

1 tbsp white vinegar

1 kg/2 lb 4 oz oxtail, cut into 2–3-cm/
  ¾–1¼-inch pieces and washed

for the stock

2 litres/3½ pints/generous 8 cups
  chicken stock

a pinch of salt

1 onion, peeled and sliced

6 coriander (cilantro) stalks

for the soup

2 onions, peeled and sliced

2 garlic cloves, peeled and pounded

1–2 cleaned Chinese celery roots
  (optional)

1 tomato, cut into wedges

1 toasted Thai cardamom pod,
  or 2 regular pods

2 Thai bay leaves, toasted, or 1 regular
  bay leaf

3-cm/1¼-inch piece of cassia bark,
  toasted

1 tsp black peppercorns, toasted and
  coarsely ground

2-cm/¾-inch piece of unpeeled galangal

2-cm/¾-inch piece of unpeeled ginger

3-cm/1¼-inch piece of dried orange peel

a pinch of salt

a pinch of sugar (optional)

nam pla (fish sauce), to taste

2–4 cayenne chillies, bruised

to serve

a handful of Vietnamese mint leaves, or
  regular mint

a handful of Thai (sawtooth) coriander
  (pointed cilantro), torn

4 small dried chillies, toasted

2 stems Chinese celery, chopped into
  3-cm/1¼-inch pieces

a good pinch of deep-fried shallots
  (see page 204)

juice of 1 lime

Fill a large saucepan with cold water and add the salt and the vinegar. Add the oxtail and bring the water up to the boil over a medium heat. As soon as it boils, remove from the heat and drain the oxtail. Refresh in some cold water and rinse. This helps to make your stock less cloudy.

Put the oxtail into a clean saucepan and cover with the chicken stock. Add the salt, onion and coriander stalks and bring to the boil. Turn down the heat and simmer, partially covered, until cooked. This will take 2–3 hours – you want the meat to be nicely tender. Skim any scum off the top as required, but keep the fat.

When cooked, remove the oxtail with a slotted spoon and set aside until cool enough to handle. Then, strip the meat from the bones (discarding the bones). Pass the stock through a fine sieve (strainer) and return to a clean saucepan. Return the meat to the stock and allow to cool completely before placing in the refrigerator for a few hours until the fat has risen to the surface and solidified.

Carefully lift off the layer of fat and set this aside before re-heating the stock over a medium heat.

For the soup, heat the solidified fat in a frying pan (skillet) or wok over a medium heat and fry the sliced onions. Add the garlic and celery roots and fry until they are beginning to colour. Pour into the simmering soup along with the fat. Add the tomato.

In a dry frying pan, toast the dry spices, along with the galangal, ginger and orange peel, then add to the soup. Season the soup with a little salt, sugar and *nam pla*, to taste. Add the bruised chillies. Skim as needed – remember to remove the scum but not the fat.

Just before serving, add the mint, coriander, dried chillies, Chinese celery and the deep-fried shallots. Squeeze in the lime juice and serve.

Moo Waan

Sweet Pork

Delicious, sticky, sweet, and topped with crispy shallots, this is an utter delight. Traditionally, this would be made with pork belly and soy sauce, but this is how I've always made it, thanks to Prayoon. It was one of Little Kay's absolute favourites.

Serve alongside fried rice, *Som Tum Thai* (Green Papaya Salad, page 174) or *Yum Mamuang* (Green Mango Salad, page 158), or just eat with freshly cooked rice and weep for joy.

Serves 4

300 g/10½ oz pork loin chops, trimmed and thinly sliced

80 g/2¾ oz palm sugar

4 tbsp *nam pla* (fish sauce)

4 Thai shallots or 2 regular shallots, peeled and sliced

2 tbsp deep-fried shallots (see page 204), to garnish

Put the pork, sugar, *nam pla*, sliced shallots and 175 ml/6 fl oz/¾ cup water into a large saucepan, then bring to the boil. Reduce the heat and simmer at a good pace for about 30 minutes, until the sauce has reduced by more than half, and become nice and sticky.

Turn out into a bowl and serve sprinkled with the crispy shallots.

Stir-fried and Deep-fried

On stir-fries

In the home kitchen, three things are critical for a successful stir-fry. Firstly, you need the right wok (see page 201). Secondly, always heat the wok and then add the cooking oil, rather than heating the oil in the wok. This ensures that the wok itself is as hot as possible, and that the oil doesn't pass its smoke point and burn. Thirdly, have your ingredients prepped and work fast!

Goong Pad Dok Guaychai

Chive Flowers Stir-fried with Prawns

This very simple stir-fry offers yet another demonstration of the fact that Thai food doesn't have to be spicy.

You can find chive flowers in most Asian supermarkets. When you buy them and cook them, the flower bud should be closed. If any have opened, de-head them and use the stems. And if you cannot find them, young fine asparagus ('sprue') works as an excellent substitute. You can also use beansprouts, in which case the dish becomes *Goong Pad Tua Gnork*.

Serves 2–4

1 tbsp vegetable oil

2 garlic cloves, finely chopped

175 g/6 oz raw prawns (shrimp), peeled

a small bunch of chive flowers, chopped into 4–5-cm/ 1½–2-inch lengths

1 tbsp caster (superfine) sugar

1 tbsp *nam pla* (fish sauce)

Heat a wok over a fairly high heat and add the oil. When the oil is hot, add the garlic and stir-fry until it's really fragrant, but not brown. Add the prawns and stir rapidly. When they begin to turn pink, add the chive flowers and continue to stir-fry for a minute or so. Add the sugar, *nam pla* and 1 tbsp water. Let that bubble up while you keep stirring for about 1–2 minutes.

Turn out on to a plate and serve.

Goong Pad Kratiam Prik Thai

Prawns Stir-fried with Garlic and Pepper

Really old Thai dishes, such as this one, do not feature chillies because chillies are not indigenous to Thailand – they were brought over by Portuguese traders in the sixteenth century. Prior to that, most flavouring and spicing was done with herbs and peppercorns. One of the particular joys of this recipe is licking the peppery fried garlic off your fingers after you've peeled the prawns – something that was actively encouraged by Prayoon, our family cook, whose recipe this is.

You can, of course, make it with ready-peeled prawns too, if you prefer.

Serves 4 as a part of a meal

12 large whole prawns (jumbo shrimp) (approx. 500 g/1 lb 2 oz)

2 tbsp *nam pla* (fish sauce)

2–3 large coriander (cilantro) roots and stems (see page 203)

1 heaped tbsp white peppercorns

6–8 garlic cloves, peeled

a pinch of salt

2 tbsp vegetable oil

In a large bowl, soak the prawns in the *nam pla* for 10 minutes.

Meanwhile, in a pestle and mortar, pound the coriander roots, white peppercorns, garlic and salt roughly together – you want some chunky bits.

Take the prawns out of the *nam pla*, shake off the excess and then roll them in the garlic, peppercorn and coriander mixture.

Heat a wok and add the oil. When the oil is very hot, pop the prawns in, a couple at a time, turning them with a spoon or spatula until they are a lovely deep orange colour and are cooked through, about 3–5 minutes, depending on their size. When each batch of the prawns are cooked, set them aside on a warm platter.

When all the prawns are cooked, take what's left of the garlicky mixture and quickly fry it off until it's crispy. Sprinkle it on top of the prawns, and serve.

Hoi Chen Pad Cha

Scallops Stir-fried with Chillies and Green Peppercorns

In all honesty, I've rarely met a shellfish I didn't like, and scallops are among my favourites – Thai scallops especially so. They are smaller than most fished in European waters, similar in fact to the queenies or queen scallops you find in the Isle of Man. If you can find them, you won't need to halve the scallop as requested below.

Krachai features here, too. It's sometimes known as 'lesser ginger', 'Chinese keys' or 'fingerroot'. It tastes like a herbaceous ginger, and it's easy to find in most Asian supermarkets. If you can't find it, make something else!

Serves 2–4

2 garlic cloves, peeled

2–4 Thai bird's eye chillies

1 tbsp vegetable oil

300 g/10½ oz scallops, roes separated and each halved into 2 discs

30 g/1 oz *krachai* (fingerroot/Chinese keys), scraped and finely slivered

1 tbsp *nam pla* (fish sauce)

1 tbsp oyster sauce

2 kaffir lime leaves, roughly torn

2 sticks fresh green peppercorns

1 long red chilli, sliced diagonally

a handful of Thai sweet basil

In a pestle and mortar, pound the garlic and bird's eye chillies together into a loose paste.

Heat a large wok and add the oil. When it's hot, add the garlic and chillies, and stir-fry until vividly fragrant. Add the scallops and the *krachai* and stir-fry until the scallops are half-cooked, then add the sauces, lime leaves, peppercorns, sliced chilli and the scallop roe, if you have it. As soon as you've stirred them in, add the basil. Stir-fry for another 30 seconds or so, then turn out on to a plate and serve.

Hoi Lai Pad Nam Prik Pao

Clams Stir-fried with Roasted Chilli Paste

For a dish that takes so little time to make, this tastes surprisingly complex. The sweet clams, rich chilli paste and fresh basil create a perfect balance of flavour. If you can't find Thai basil, you can use regular basil instead.

Serves 2-4 as a part of a meal

500 g/1 lb 2 oz clams

2 tbsp vegetable oil

2–3 garlic cloves, peeled and chopped

1 tbsp *nam prik pao* (roasted chilli paste, see page 203)

1 tbsp *nam pla* (fish sauce)

1 tsp caster (superfine) sugar

2 long red chillies, sliced diagonally

a handful of Thai sweet basil leaves

In a colander, rinse the clams well under cold running water, discarding any open ones that refuse to close after a firm tap with the back of a knife.

On a high heat, heat the wok until it's very hot and add the oil. Add the garlic and fry until golden. Add the clams and the *nam prik pao*, and stir-fry for 1–2 minutes.

One at a time, add the *nam pla*, sugar, 2 tbsp water and the chillies, stirring them in well after each addition. Continue to cook, stirring all the time, until all the clams have opened (discard any that remain closed).

Finally, add most of the basil and stir it in until wilted.

Serve at once, with the last few basil leaves scattered over the top.

~ *There are so many brands of* nam prik pao *on the market and it will keep in the fridge for ages. My preferred brand is Mae Pranom. As a kid, I used to eat it spread on thick white bread... Try it!* ~

Hua Kalumpee Tod Nam Pla

Cabbage Stir-fried with Fish Sauce

This is one of the first dishes I learned to cook – simple and delicious. And saw me through many a term as an impecunious drama student.

Serves 4–6

400–450 g/14 oz–1 lb cabbage (white, Savoy, spring, January King… whatever's to hand)
2 tbsp vegetable oil
4–6 garlic cloves, peeled and chopped
2 tbsp *nam pla* (fish sauce)
½ tsp caster (superfine) sugar (optional)

Core the cabbage, remove any tough outer leaves and cut it into chunks. Separate the leaves, then rinse in cold water and set aside to dry.

Heat a wok over a high heat, and then add the oil. When it's hot, add the garlic and stir-fry until fragrant and just about to turn golden. Add the cabbage and stir-fry in its residual water, coating it with the garlic. Add the *nam pla*, pouring it around the cabbage on to the hot wok – you want to get a real hit of that funky smell and some caramelization. Continue to stir-fry the cabbage through the fish sauce until it's softening slightly and 'catching'. Add the sugar, if using. Give it all a final toss and add a little more *nam pla* or a dash of water, if you think it needs it.

Serve with Thai jasmine rice.

Mara Pad Kai

Stir-fried Bitter Melon with Eggs

What could be simpler or more delicious than scrambled eggs? Here's a Thai version, where the creamy egg is juxtaposed with the crunch of bitter melon (bitter gourd).

Serves 2–4

2 eggs

a few dashes of soy sauce

a good grinding of white pepper

2 tbsp vegetable oil

250 g/9 oz bitter melon (bitter gourd), deseeded, quartered and cut into slices

In a bowl, beat the eggs lightly with the soy and the white pepper. Set aside.

Heat a wok over high heat, and add the oil. Add the bitter melon, and stir-fry. Keep going until the melon starts to soften a little. Add the eggs and scramble through the bitter melon until cooked to your liking. I prefer a softer scramble, but you can go for something firmer, an omelette-style if you like, flipping it halfway through.

Pad Pak
Ruan Mit

Stir-fried Mixed Vegetables in Oyster Sauce and Garlic

When I say mixed vegetables, I mean mixed vegetables – you can throw in pretty much anything you have in the bottom of the fridge. I like baby corn, mangetout (snow peas), cabbage and green beans.

Serves 4 as part of a meal

1 tbsp light soy sauce
1 tbsp oyster sauce
a pinch of caster (superfine) sugar
200 g/7 oz mixed vegetables
2 tbsp vegetable oil
4 garlic cloves, chopped
1 large red chilli, sliced

In a small bowl, mix the soy and oyster sauce together with the sugar, and put it where you can reach it quickly when you're cooking. Then, rinse the vegetables, but don't dry.

Turn your largest hob ring/burner to maximum, and heat your wok until it's almost smoking. Add the oil, and when it's good and hot, add the garlic and the chilli. Stir-fry until the garlic turns a golden nutty brown. Add the wet vegetables, hardest first, and stir vigorously. As the veg begins to wilt, add the mixed sauces and continue stir-frying.

The vegetables should be wilting in the hot sauce and their residual water; if not, add another dash of water, and continue stir-frying until they're cooked to your liking and well coated in the sauce, garlic and chilli, about 3 minutes or so.

Turn out on to a plate and serve.

~ When stir-frying, always have a glass or mug of water or light stock standing by – just in case you need to add a dash. ~

Pad Pak Boong Fai Daeng

Stir-fried Morning Glory

This could be my favourite Thai vegetable dish of all. It's made in broadly the same way all over the country but, as ever, some cooks have their own little tweaks. At my friend Khun Thip's restaurant Chao Lay in Hua Hin, chef Khun Nai adds a fistful of peeled, whole, tiny Thai garlic cloves, which is simply heavenly.

One of the difficulties, however, for the home cook, is that we don't generally have the chance to cook on charcoal braziers or even over the brutally fierce gas wok hobs that you can plug into a gas canister. So, we can't easily ignite the oil in the dish to introduce that delicious 'flamed' flavour into the sauce – *fai daeng* means 'red flame' – and it's the real secret to the dish.

Serves 4 as part of a meal

4 small garlic cloves, peeled

1 long red or orange chilli

2 Thai bird's eye chillies, optional

a pinch of salt

2 tbsp vegetable oil

200 g/7 oz morning glory, trimmed and chopped into 5-cm/2-inch pieces

1 tsp caster (superfine) sugar

2 tbsp oyster sauce

3 tbsp yellow beans, rinsed

2 tbsp water or stock (if needed)

In a pestle and mortar, pound together the garlic, chilli and a pinch of salt. Set aside.

Heat a wok over a high heat and add the oil. Once the oil is hot, add the garlic and chilli paste, and stir-fry until it's fragrant and golden. Add the morning glory and continue stir-frying for a minute or two.

Add the sugar, oyster sauce, yellow beans and a splash of stock or water, stirring after each addition.

Move everything around the wok (try to catch some red flame!) until it's bubbling fiercely, the leaves are wilted and the stems *al dente*. If it looks a little dry at any point, add another splash of stock or water.

Serve.

~ If you want to make this vegetarian or vegan, you can substitute the oyster sauce for a mixture of 1½ tbsp light soy and 1½ tbsp dark soy. ~

A Quick Digression About Elephants

I've said this before: you don't know your place in the world until you walk beside an elephant, the true king of the jungle, and so integral to Thai culture that one used to feature on the country's flag.

And yet, despite this, there are now only about 3,000 of them left in the wild, and just over 3,500 in domesticity. The species is in trouble. And it's the humans' fault.

I struggle with the human/elephant conundrum. We have created a world that has little room for them in the wild. And even though humans have worked with elephants for almost as long as they have with horses, there is still outrageous bad practice and cruelty involved.

I write this as one who rescued an orphaned male back in 1993 when he was just 5 years old. He's 30 now, named Bo-That, over 3 metres/10 feet tall, and living at the Thai Elephant Conservation Centre in Lampang, where he's cared for by his *kwan*, Tam.

Do I like that he's in captivity? No. I do not. But I also know that he would be dead if he wasn't. I know too, that most elephant sanctuaries only take in females because they're easier – Bo-That's in musth half the time, and 5,000 kg/5½ tons of rage and crazy is damned dangerous to be near. At Lampang, they don't discriminate. And, aligned to the Conservation Centre, they have the world's leading elephant hospital, where they have pioneered elephant C-sections and prostheses. He's in the best place he can be. And Tam adores him.

The sad truth is that elephants – Asian and African – will not survive without our help. And the Asian elephant's plight is by far the worse. So what can we do?

Encourage better husbandry, for one. At Lampang, they endorse the work of Dr. Andrew Mclean's Human Elephant Learning Program (HELP) which, following the example of horse-whispers like Buck Brannaman and Warwick Schiller, re-teaches *kwan*s and mahouts how to work with their elephants across Asia. And by supporting elephant charities: my favourite is The Golden Triangle Asian Elephant Foundation (www.helpingelephants.org) who do an extraordinary job.

I love my beautiful boy. He's grumpy. According to Tam, he only likes him and me, and tolerates everyone else. And chaps like him are vital to the species's survival.

Hoi Tod

Oyster Omelette

This is a street-food staple, made in massive pans in night markets all across Thailand. It's very simple to make a home version, too. I've cut back heavily on the oil – making it more of a scramble than a true Thai omelette – because I find that, with less grease, the oysters' flavour has more room to shine.

Serves 2, or 4 as a part of a larger meal

12 oysters, shucked and drained
rice flour, for dredging
4 eggs
1½ tsp *nam pla* (fish sauce)
freshly ground white pepper
1 tbsp picked coriander (cilantro) leaves
2 tbsp vegetable oil
100 g/3½ oz beansprouts
2 spring onions (scallions), cut into
   1.5-cm/½-inch batons
½ long red chilli, finely sliced

Dredge the oysters in the rice flour and set aside.

Beat the eggs together with the *nam pla*, pepper and half of the coriander leaves.

Heat a well-seasoned wok and add the oil. When it's hot, add the oysters and cook for about 1 minute. Pour in the egg and add the beansprouts and half of the spring onions. Cook, stirring the egg from the outside in, until you have a scramble-omelette hybrid. The texture should be just firm.

Turn out on to a plate and garnish with the remaining spring onion, coriander leaves and the sliced chilli.

Serve at once with *Nam Pla Prik* (Fish Sauce with Chillies, page 193) and/or Sriracha sauce.

Moo Pad Khing

Pork Stir-fried with Ginger

There's a strong Chinese influence in this simple stir-fry. It's fragrant and delicious, and perfect for a quick supper on its own, with rice. In which case, this recipe makes enough for two. That said, I most often serve it in the context of a larger meal because of its relative mildness.

Serves 4 as a part of a meal

2 tbsp vegetable oil

3 garlic cloves, peeled and chopped

300 g/10½ oz pork, thinly sliced for stir-frying

50 g/2 oz ginger, peeled and slivered

2 tbsp light soy sauce

1–2 tbsp oyster sauce

a dash of *nam pla* (fish sauce)

1 tbsp stock or water

a pinch of caster (superfine) sugar

freshly ground white pepper

1 large red chilli, sliced diagonally, to garnish

2 spring onions (scallions), sliced diagonally, to garnish

Heat the wok over a very high heat. When it's hot, add the oil, followed by the garlic. Stir-fry until fragrant and almost golden, then add the pork. Stir-fry until the pork is almost cooked, then add most of the ginger, stirring it through, and add the liquids and the sugar. Stir-fry for 1 minute or long enough to bring the sauce together. Remove from the heat, season with white pepper to taste, and turn out on to a serving plate.

Garnish with the chilli, spring onions and the few reserved slivers of fresh ginger, and serve.

Pad Krapow Moo

Pork Stir-fried with
Holy Basil

This is one of my favourite things to eat in the world, especially when served *lart khao kai dao*, as a one-dish meal over rice with a deep-fried egg to top it off. It is one of the first Thai recipes I learned to cook. Even so, I wasn't surprised to receive a text from David Thompson when he read my version, that said: 'Beans?! Beans!! If you were here now…'

This is something of a running joke between us, because – like many chefs – David is a purist, and rightly revered for his knowledge of Thai food. He was referring to a version of *pad krapow* made solely with *nam pla*. No soy and certainly no green beans. And he is both right and wrong.

There are no Larousse-like standard recipe texts in Thai cooking. Instead, as with Italian food, there's enormous variation not only regionally but from cook to cook. And nowhere is this better demonstrated than with *pad krapow*.

I picked up the offending version from a road-side cook in Kanchanaburi. I like the deep savoury qualities given by the soy and the texture of the green beans. I also like the 'pure' fish sauce version David and I like to argue about. So I include both (see overleaf).

I most frequently make this with pork, but you can use beef, chicken, prawns (shrimp), duck, tofu, mushrooms, you name it. You can even use the *Moo Grop* (Crispy Thai Pork Belly, page 129). And, while you really should finely chop up the meat yourself, when I make this for my lunch, I just buy minced (ground) pork from the supermarket!

Serves 2 *lart khao*, or 4 as a part of a larger meal

Recipe continues overleaf.

Pad Krapow Moo continued

4–6 Thai bird's eye chillies

1 large red chilli, cut into chunks

6 garlic cloves, peeled

a pinch of sea salt

2 tbsp dark soy sauce

2 tbsp light soy sauce

a pinch of caster (superfine) sugar

2 tbsp vegetable oil

300 g/10½ oz pork, minced (ground)

100 g/3½ oz green beans, topped, tailed and cut into 1-cm/½-inch pieces

a very large handful of holy basil leaves – the more the merrier (see tip)

In a pestle and mortar, pound the chillies, garlic and salt to a rough paste. Set aside.

In a small bowl, mix the soy sauces and 2 tbsp water, and stir in the sugar.

Heat a wok until its really hot, then add the oil. Throw in the chilli-garlic paste and stir-fry for a few seconds – until you can really smell everything in the pan, but not long enough to colour the garlic. Now add the pork and stir-fry until it's cooked through, then add the green beans.

Add the liquid and stir through, allowing it to bubble up before adding nearly all the basil and letting it wilt into the dish.

Serve over steamed jasmine rice, with *Kai Dao* (Deep-fried Eggs, page 133), as pictured, and the remaining basil leaves scattered on top.

~ *If you can't find holy basil* (bai krapow), *you can use Thai sweet basil instead. Worst-case scenario, I have even made this with regular basil – but it isn't quite the same. If you do, just don't call it* Pad Krapow. ~

Pad Krapow Moo with Nam Pla

4–6 Thai bird's eye chillies

1 large red chilli, cut into chunks

6 garlic cloves, peeled

a pinch of sea salt

2 tbsp vegetable oil

300 g/10½ oz pork, minced (ground)

3 tbsp *nam pla* (fish sauce)

1 tsp caster (superfine) sugar

a very large handful of holy basil leaves (see tip, above)

Pound the paste together as above. Then fry it off in the hot oil, followed by the meat, also as above. When it is almost cooked, add the *nam pla* and the sugar. Stir-fry together until amalgamated and the pork is cooked. Then add most of the basil and wilt it into the dish. Serve as above.

Pad Normai

Stir-fried Bamboo Shoots with Pork

Should you head out on to the Thai streets between five and six in the evening, as all the young professionals hurry home from work, you will find plenty of *khao gaeng* stalls along the route. This is not street food, in the sense that they're not cooking it on the street – it is often made elsewhere. And while these stalls may have a couple of tables, most people will take the food home for dinner.

The last time I was in Bangkok, I had this dish off a *khao gaeng* stall on Soi Saladaeng as I, too, was hurrying back from some appointments. I thought, as I ate it, 'why don't I make this more often?' Now I do. You can vary the heat in it, depending on what you want to serve it with, or simply have it on rice.

I favour the vacuum-packed bamboo shoots for this. Preparing the fresh stuff takes a couple of hours, and the canned slivered shoots always disappoint.

Serves 4 as a part of a meal

3 garlic cloves, peeled

3–5 red Thai bird's eye chillies

2 tbsp vegetable oil

125 g/4½ oz minced (ground) pork

200 g/7 oz bamboo shoots, cut into thin strips

2 tbsp *nam pla* (fish sauce)

a pinch of caster (superfine) sugar

2–3 kaffir lime leaves, finely sliced

In a pestle and mortar, pound the garlic and chillies together into a rough paste.

Heat a wok over a high heat and add the oil. When it's hot, add the garlic and chilli mixture, and cook until fragrant and the garlic is just beginning to turn a light gold. Add the pork and cook until you no longer see any pink meat. Add the bamboo shoots, the *nam pla* and the sugar, and stir-fry for another 30 seconds or so, until the bamboo shoots are hot through. Finally, add the kaffir lime leaves, stir through, and turn the dish out on to a serving plate.

Yai's Moo Khem

Yai's Recipe for Salty Pork

This is incredibly easy to make, and is the ideal accompaniment for the *Gaeng Leung* (Southern Spicy Sour Curry, page 75). If you have any left over, add a tablespoon to a *Kai Jeow* (Thai Omelette, page 134) or serve it cold, on the side, with the omelette and some freshly steamed rice.

Photographed on page 126, bottom left.

Serves 2–4

2–3 garlic cloves, peeled and finely chopped

2 tbsp yellow beans, rinsed

1 tbsp vegetable oil

250 g/9 oz minced (ground) pork

1 tbsp oyster sauce

1 tbsp light soy sauce

a pinch of caster (superfine) sugar

Mix the garlic and the yellow beans together in a bowl.

Place the wok over a high heat and, when it's hot, add the oil. When it's hot, add the garlic and yellow beans and give them a quick turn around the oil. Add the pork, stirring it into the mixture until it starts to take colour, then add all the rest of the ingredients. Stir-fry until the pork is cooked through, brown and fragrant.

Pad Sator

'Stink Beans' Stir-fried with Pork and Prawns

A Southern favourite, *sator* (or 'stink beans') have a very, erm, pronounced taste. Nutty and slightly peppery, they also have a distinct smell. They are delicious, but… perhaps they're best eaten with friends! If you can't get *sator* you could use broad (fava) beans or sliced runner beans, but it's the unique texture and flavour of the stink bean that makes the dish.

This is a Southern dish, and it's one of the rare occasions where I've pulled my punch on the chilli. If you want to go for it, think in terms of 6–8 Thai bird's eye chillies instead of 4–6.

Photographed on page 126, middle left.

Serves 2–4

½ tsp roasted chilli paste

½ tsp good-quality red curry paste

1 tbsp *kapi* (shrimp paste)

4–6 garlic cloves, peeled and coarsely chopped

4–6 Thai bird's eye chillies, coarsely chopped

2 tbsp vegetable oil

150 g/5½ oz pork steak, thinly sliced into strips

60 g/2 oz *sator* beans ('stink beans'), halved lengthways

80 g/3 oz raw prawns (shrimp), peeled

1 tsp *nam pla* (fish sauce)

a good squeeze of lime juice

4–5 kaffir lime leaves, shredded

1 tsp caster (superfine) sugar

1 tbsp coconut cream (optional), to serve

Mix the chilli paste, curry paste and the *kapi* together in a small bowl and set aside.

Roughly crush the garlic and the chillies in a pestle and mortar, then stir in the shrimp paste mix until well combined.

Place the wok over a high heat and, when it's hot, add the oil. When it's hot, add the chilli and shrimp paste mixture and stir-fry until fragrant, just 1 minute or so. Add the pork and stir-fry until cooked through – if you think it's looking a bit dry, add a splash of water.

Keep on stirring while you add the *sator* and the prawns. Then add the fish sauce, a dash of lime juice, the lime leaves and sugar, and carry on stirring for a couple of minutes or so. Again, if it starts looking too dry at any point, just add a splash of water. Taste and adjust the seasoning.

Place on a serving platter and spoon or drizzle the coconut cream (if using) over the top.

Three Stir-fries with Pak Khana

Pak khana is also known as Chinese broccoli, and is easy to find in most Asian supermarkets. I especially like it because the leaves wilt and catch the sauce beautifully while the stems retain bite and texture. Here are three broadly similar ways to cook it.

Photographed on page 127, bottom right.

Serves 2–6

Pad Pak Khana Namman Hoi

Stir-fried Chinese Broccoli with Oyster Sauce

2 tbsp vegetable oil

3 garlic cloves, peeled and chopped or 6 Thai garlic cloves, squashed whole in skin

1 large red chilli, sliced (optional)

200 g/7 oz *pak khana* (Chinese broccoli), trimmed, sliced and washed

1 tbsp light soy sauce

1 tbsp oyster sauce

½ tsp caster (superfine) sugar

Heat a wok over a high heat and add the oil. When it's hot, add the garlic and chilli, and stir-fry until the garlic begins to colour. Add the *pak khana* and stir-fry, mixing it together with the chilli and garlic. After 1 minute or so, add the soy and oyster sauces, sugar and a splash of water, and continue stir-frying until cooked.

Pad Pak Khana Moo Grop

Stir-fried Chinese Broccoli with Crispy Pork

2 tbsp vegetable oil

3 garlic cloves, peeled and chopped or 6 Thai garlic cloves, squashed whole in skin

1 large red chilli, sliced

200 g/7 oz *pak khana* (Chinese broccoli), trimmed, sliced and washed

1 tbsp light soy sauce

1 tbsp oyster sauce

1½ tsp white vinegar

½ tsp caster (superfine) sugar

200 g/7 oz *Moo Grop* (Crispy Thai Pork Belly, page 129), cubed

Heat a wok over a high heat and add the oil. When it's hot, add the garlic and chilli, and stir-fry until the garlic begins to colour. Add the *pak khana* and stir-fry, mixing it together with the chilli and garlic. After 1 minute or so, add the soy and oyster sauces, the vinegar, sugar and a splash of water, and continue stir-frying until the *pak khana* is almost cooked. Add the pork and stir it through to heat, but not so much that you lose its crispiness, then serve.

Pad Pak Khana
Pla Kem

Stir-fried Chinese Broccoli with Salted Fish

100 g/3½ oz *pla kem* (salted mackerel) (see tip)

2 tbsp vegetable oil

3 garlic cloves, peeled and chopped or 6 Thai garlic cloves, squashed whole in skin

1 large red chilli, sliced

200 g/7 oz *pak khana* (Chinese broccoli), trimmed, sliced and washed

1 tbsp light soy sauce

1 tbsp oyster sauce

½ tsp caster (superfine) sugar

Skin and remove the bones from the salted fish, and cut it into small slices.

Heat a non-stick pan over a low–medium heat and dry-fry the fish until it's golden brown and crumbly. Set aside to cool. You can do this step well in advance.

Heat a wok over a high heat and add the oil. When it's hot, add the garlic and chilli, and stir-fry until the garlic begins to colour. Add the *pak khana* and stir-fry, mixing it together with the chilli and garlic. After 1 minute or so, add the soy and oyster sauces, sugar and a splash of water, and continue stir-frying until the *pak khana* is cooked. (I often pre-mix the sauces, sugar and a splash of water in one little pot – it makes it so much easier when I'm stir-frying.) Finally, add the salted fish, stir it in well, and serve.

~ *You can buy* pla kem, *or salted mackerel, in most Asian supermarkets. It tends to come vacuum-packed, in slices that are 1 cm/½ inch thick. I find that one of these slices is enough to make this recipe twice, so I take what I need and refrigerate the rest.* ~

Kap Moo

Pork Scratchings

Yes, yes... of course you can buy them in shops, but they are often salted to the point of no return. Bleugh! And I say that as one who loves salt. Better to make them at home. It's a good thing that this is such an easy recipe – you just need a friendly butcher who will save all his excess pork skin for you.

I haven't added precise quantities here, because you never really know how much you're going to get. This last time was a bit of a win-win – I got 2 pieces of about 9 x 20 cm/3½ x8 inches, which I then halved.

pork skin
salt
vegetable oil, for deep-frying

Begin by trimming as much of the fat off the pork skin as you can. Then pop it into a pan of well-salted boiling water, cover and simmer until it's cooked. This takes about 1–1½ hours.

Remove the skin from the water and drain thoroughly on paper towels. Pat it dry, and let it cool for about 10 minutes, until you can handle it without burning yourself. Now, scrape off as much of the remaining fat as possible. I use a spoon. You can then either leave it in the fridge overnight to really dry out, or just leave it to dry for a couple of hours.

Preheat the oven to the lowest possible setting (50°C/120°F). Place the pork skin on a rack over a baking tray and leave it in the oven, turning it occasionally, for 24 hours. When it's done, it should be hard and almost translucent, like a piece of amber glass.

Remove from the oven and let it cool. You can now store it in an airtight box or sealed bag until you want to use it.

Heat some oil in a wok until very hot. Break the skin into shards and fry a few at a time until puffed and crispy.

Scoop out and drain on paper towels, seasoning with a little salt while still hot.

Serve with the *Nam Prik Num* (Grilled Chilli and Aubergine Relish, page 196).

Moo Grop

Crispy Thai Pork Belly

This is not so much a dish in itself, but an ingredient for other things. You might slice it thinly and serve it with the rice and dipping sauce you'll find in the recipe for *Khao Mun Gai* (Thai-Hunanese Chicken and Rice, page 45); or cut it into chunks to use as the protein component of a *Pad Krapow* (Holy Basil Stir-Fry, page 118). My favourite thing is to stir-fry it, cut into chunks or slices, with *pak khana* (Chinese broccoli, page 124). Even better, you can make it a couple of days before you need it.

Photographed on page 126, top left.

Makes 400 g/14 oz

400 g/14 oz pork belly, boned and in one piece, skin un-scored

1 tbsp salt, plus extra for salting the cooking water

1 tbsp white vinegar

vegetable oil, for deep-frying

Clean the pork, and boil it in salted water for about 1 hour, until soft. Set aside to cool.

Once it is cool enough to handle, cut crosses in the skin (but not so deep that you cut the flesh). Mix the 1 tablespoon of salt and vinegar together, and rub into the cuts. Leave to dry for as long as possible (you are trying to replicate drying it in the Thai sun). I tend to leave it uncovered in the fridge overnight.

Heat the oil in a stable wok or deep-fat fryer to 170°C/340°F and deep-fry the pork until the skin is crispy and golden. It should take 5–8 minutes, depending on the thickness of the pork. Set aside to drain on paper towels.

Moo Nork Kok

'Pigs Outside Their Sty'

This recipe has been 25 years in the making. I first had *moo nork kok* at The Fern Restaurant in Mae Hong Son, when I was working on the movie *Operation Dumbo Drop* back in the early '90s. I became obsessed with it – so much so, that I ordered it every time we went there, which is a lot, because we were up there for 5 months and there weren't that many places to eat. But I never got the recipe. I couldn't find anyone else who knew how to make it. It got to the point that I began to wonder if I'd imagined the dish altogether until I found a guy in Thai Town, Los Angeles, who said he knew the dish but didn't have the recipe.

I remained undeterred. As soon as this book started coming together, I knew it had to feature *moo nork kok*, so I went back to Mae Hong Son, and The Fern specifically, to find it. I ate it every day for four days, asking the staff about the recipe each time.

The cooked rice semi-cures the pork, lending it a sharp, almost lemony tang.

Here it is.

Serves 2–4

6 garlic cloves, peeled
1 tsp salt
6 tbsp cooked rice
300 g/10½ oz pork steak, cut into thin strips
vegetable oil, for deep-frying

In a pestle and mortar, pound the garlic and the salt together, then add the rice and pound again until you have a rough paste. Mix the pork through the paste. Put it all in a sealable bag or Tupperware container and refrigerate for 48 hours.

When you're ready to cook, heat the oil in a wok or deep-fryer set to 170°C/340°F. Fry the pork, still covered in paste, until the rice is crisp and golden and the pork is cooked through.

Serve with batons of raw cucumber, steamed winged beans, finely sliced ginger, pickled garlic and *Nam Jim Jaew* (Roasted Chilli Dipping Sauce, page 194), as pictured.

Not Soi Polo Chicken

Deep-fried Chicken Inspired by Soi Polo Restaurant

Like many before me, I have tried to prise the recipe from Khun Jae Kee at the Soi Polo Fried Chicken restaurant. And like every one of them, I have failed. I can tell you many reasons why theirs is so special – its sheer deliciousness, its lack of greasiness, the lashings of deep-fried garlic that come with it, the dipping sauce – and I can do my level best to replicate it. To do so, I travelled to Hat Yai in southern Thailand, which is pretty much ground zero for Thai fried chicken, to pick up a few tips, and ate more fried chicken that I had previously thought possible. I do it all for you, dear reader...

Serves 4–6

1 x 1.5-kg/3 lb 5-oz chicken, jointed into 8 pieces

1 batch of *Gai Yang* marinade (see page 140)

3 litres/5 pints/13 cups vegetable oil, for deep frying

1 batch of deep-fried garlic or deep-fried shallot (page 204), to serve

for the batter

100 g/3½ oz/¾ cup rice flour

100 g/3½ oz/¾ cup plain (all-purpose) flour

1 tsp baking powder

350 ml/12 fl oz/1½ cups cold water

a dash of *nam pla* (fish sauce) or a good pinch of salt

Marinate the chicken for as long as possible – you can get away with 1 hour, but ideally you want to give it 24 hours.

When you're ready to cook, make the batter. In a large bowl, thoroughly mix the flours and baking powder. Add the cold water and *nam pla* or salt, and whisk until you have a smooth batter.

Heat the oil in a wok or deep-fryer to 170°C/340°F. If using the former, the oil has reached temperature when a cube of bread will fry to a good golden brown in just under 1 minute.

Stir the chicken through the batter mixture. Allow the excess to run off before using tongs to carefully submerge the pieces in the hot oil. Fry for 7–10 minutes, until cooked through, setting the pieces aside on paper towels as you go. I tend to fry 2 pieces at a time to ensure the oil doesn't lose too much temperature. Note that the fried chicken will be a deep mahogany colour. This is because the sugars in the marinade caramelize as the chicken cooks, not because you've burnt it.

Serve, covered with deep-fried garlic or shallot.

Kai Dao

Deep-fried Eggs

Simply put, this is nothing more than an egg poached in a wok of hot oil. Why? Because there's nothing better than cutting that yolk open, and letting it dribble down on to fried rice or a plate of rice with *Pad Krapow* (Holy Basil Stir-fry, page 118).

Makes as many as you require

300 ml/10 fl oz/1¼ cups vegetable oil
eggs (as many as you require)

In a small wok, heat the oil until it's as hot as you dare. Then, crack in an egg – be careful, it will spit – and cook, basting in the oil, until the white is crispy at the edges but the yolk within remains runny. Set aside on paper towels. Bring the oil back to its full, furious heat, and repeat as often as necessary.

~ Make two of these, plate them and dress with a basic yum dressing (see page 158) and you'll have a yum kai dao. ~

Kai Jeow

Thai Omelette

A lot of Thais like to eat this kind of simple omelette with a meal, but you will rarely find it on a menu because it's assumed that every cook knows how to make one. It acts as a neutral foil to the other dishes on the table. On its own, with rice and a dot of Sriracha sauce, it's also excellent comfort food.

Bear in mind that this is completely unlike a European or American omelette. You are almost deep-frying it in the wok, which gives it a fluffy texture; you don't fold it in on itself; and you flip the whole thing over in its cooking oil to complete cooking, not unlike a Spanish tortilla.

Serves 2–4 as part of a meal

3 eggs

freshly ground white pepper

1 spring onion (scallion), finely sliced
   diagonally

1–2 tbsp minced (ground) pork or
   white crab meat (optional)

a squeeze of lime juice

1 tbsp *nam pla* (fish sauce)

90 ml/3 fl oz/⅓ cup vegetable oil

fresh coriander (cilantro) leaves,
   to garnish

In a small bowl, beat the eggs lightly together with the white pepper, spring onion, the pork or crab, if using (if you are, make sure the meat is well distributed through the egg), and the lime juice. Then add the *nam pla*, and beat it in too. Set aside.

Heat a wok over the highest heat until it's smoking. Then add the oil, and heat until it shimmers – get it as hot as you dare. Add the eggs and cook until they begin to set, then turn the whole omelette – its base should be invitingly golden-brown – and cook for a further 20 seconds or so. Don't worry if it breaks; it doesn't have to be neat, and the last bit of cooking will bind it together.

Remove from the hot oil to drain on paper towels (you might also want to blot the top). Then plate it, garnished with coriander leaves, and serve at once.

Two Ways With Fried Fish

A whole fried fish is something of a statement dish, and always proves popular. There must be over a hundred slight regional variations all across Thailand. I've had a deep-fried snakehead fish in Kanchaburi, smothered in a rich tamarind and cashew nut sauce; tiny crispy cotton fish in Khon Kaen with a dipping sauce; and deep-fried bass in *gaeng som* in Chiang Mai, which you can easily make using the recipe on page 82, leaving out the prawns (shrimp) and the omelette, and using the frying method here.

Serves 4

How to fry the fish

for the fish

1 sea bass, tilapia, snapper, sea bream or mullet (about 1 kg/2 lb 4 oz), gutted and scaled

1 tbsp *nam pla* (fish sauce)

vegetable oil, for frying

Cut diagonal slashes in both sides of the fish, then marinate it in the *nam pla* for about 10 minutes.

Meanwhile, make either of the sauces below or overleaf.

When you're ready to fry, dry the fish thoroughly with paper towels. Heat 8–10 cm/3–4 inches of oil in a wok to 180°C/350°F, then fry the fish gently until it's golden brown and cooked through – how long this takes will depend on the size of your fish. Set aside to drain on paper towels while you finish the sauce.

Pla Tod Nam Pla

Fried Fish in a *Nam Pla* Sauce

for the *nam pla* sauce

4 tbsp palm sugar

4 tbsp *nam pla* (fish sauce)

In small saucepan over a low heat, entirely dissolve the palm sugar in 4 tbsp water, then bring it to the boil. Add the *nam pla*, stir to combine, then remove from the heat.

Fry the fish as above. When it has drained of excess oil, place the fish on a warm platter and either pour the sauce over the top or serve it in a small bowl on the side.

Serve with the *Yum Mamuang* (Green Mango Salad, page 158) on the side, omitting the deep-fried squid or fish and stirring 3–4 chopped fresh Thai bird's eye chillies through it instead.

Pla Tod
Sam Rot

Three-flavoured Fried Fish

for the paste
2 tbsp coriander (cilantro) root
   (see page 203), chopped
a pinch of sea salt
4 long fresh chillies, deseeded
   and chopped
4 garlic cloves, peeled
4 Thai shallots or 2 regular shallots,
   peeled

for the sauce
1 tbsp vegetable oil
125 g/4½ oz palm sugar
2 tbsp tamarind paste (purée)
2 tbsp *nam pla* (fish sauce)

to garnish
2 long dried red chillies
a handful of Thai basil

In a pestle and mortar, pound together the paste ingredients in the order listed until smooth.

Heat a wok over a medium heat, then add the oil. When it's hot, fry the paste until fragrant, about 1 minute or so. Then, add the palm sugar, tamarind paste and the *nam pla*. Stir together until the sugar has dissolved, adding 2 tbsp water if the sauce looks dry. Taste for balance – it should be sweet, sour, hot and salty – then remove from the heat and set aside.

Fry the fish according to the method on page 135, then deep-fry the garnish ingredients until the leaves are crispy. Drain on paper towels.

To serve, place the fish on a warm platter. Pour the sauce over the fish, then crush the fried chillies and scatter them with the basil leaves over the top.

Khun Nai's Pla Muk Tod Kratiem from Chao Lay

Squid Deep-fried with Garlic and White Pepper

Hua Hin has changed a lot since I was small. Where once it was a sleepy seaside town with one glorious old-fashioned hotel, it is now a heaving resort with hundreds of condos, hotels, and girly bars. It's changed so much that now I have just three reasons to go there.

The first is its fantastic covered day market, Chat Chai, right in the centre of town, where I frequently go to stock up on dried shrimp and the best palm sugar I have found anywhere in the world. The second is Baan Bayan, a boutique hotel in a buttercup yellow, early twentieth-century house, which remains one of my favourite places to unwind, and which has an adorable cat called Cheese. And the third is Chao Lay, a restaurant that juts out into the sea on a pier.

I have been coming to Chao Lay for as long as I can remember. The seafood is excellent, the waiters have a charming piratical swagger, and the owners are friends. What's not to like?

I love this dish so much that I order it practically every time I visit. The chef Khun Nai thought I ought to have the recipe.

Serves 2, or 4 as a part of a larger Thai meal

2 squid (about 25–30 cm/10–12 inches long), cleaned and cut into rings
2 heaped tbsp roughly chopped garlic
1 heaped tsp stock (bouillon) powder
1 tbsp light soy sauce
2 heaped tsp ground white pepper
2 heaped tbsp plain (all-purpose) flour
vegetable oil, for deep-frying
deep-fried garlic (page 204), to serve (optional)

Put the squid into a bowl, and add the garlic, stock powder, soy sauce and pepper. Mix lightly but thoroughly with your hands. Add the flour, and lightly mix again with your hands.

In a large deep wok, heat enough vegetable oil for deep-frying until hot. Using your hands, carefully separate the squid pieces and put them into your frying basket or ladle. Lower the squid into the hot fat, and deep-fry for about 2 minutes, moving the squid in the fat to make sure it cooks evenly, until it is crisp and golden.

Drain on paper towels and pat dry.

If you like, serve with some deep-fried garlic scattered on top.

Grilled,
Steamed
and Baked

Classic Gai Yang

Grilled Chicken

Grilled chicken is insanely popular in Thailand. There are stalls selling it all across the country from the Andaman Coast to the Lao border, all slightly different, all equally delicious, and everyone has their favourites. While I love SP Chicken in Chiang Mai and Gai Yang Rabeab in Khon Kaen, my favourite is Khun Tee's roadside stall in Chiang Dao, which is – as the *Michelin Guide* would say – worth a detour.

Khun Tee brines his chicken prior to grilling. I've done my best to replicate it here. I also include a marinade. If you brine the chicken, use the marinade as a baste while you're cooking. Otherwise, marinate the chicken for at least one hour, ideally six.

Serves 4–6

1 x 1.5-kg/3 lb 5-oz chicken, spatchcocked

for the brine
3 litres/5 pints/13 cups water

1 tsp white peppercorns, lightly crushed

1 tsp coriander seeds, lightly crushed

3–4 large garlic cloves

125 g/4½ oz/½ cup salt

50 g/1¾ oz/¼ cup caster (superfine) sugar

for the marinade
4–6 garlic cloves

1 tbsp white peppercorns

4 coriander (cilantro) roots (see page 203)

1 tbsp palm sugar

1 tbsp *nam pla* (fish sauce)

1 tbsp light soy sauce

a splash of vegetable oil

a good pinch of salt

To make the brine, combine all the ingredients together in a large bowl, making sure that the sugar and salt have completely dissolved. Immerse the chicken in the brine for a good 6 hours. Then remove it and pat dry before cooking.

To make the marinade, pound the garlic, peppercorns and coriander root together in a pestle and mortar until you have a paste. Then stir in the remaining ingredients until they're well combined.

If you are not brining the chicken, rub all the marinade on to it and leave for as long as you can. If you have brined the chicken, reserve the marinade to baste the chicken as it cooks .

To cook, barbecue (grill) the chicken to the side of banked coals, turning from time to time, until cooked through and the juices run clear. This should take 45 minutes–1 hour, depending on the chicken and the barbecue.

Alternatively, roast the chicken in an oven preheated to 180°C fan/200°C/400°F/gas mark 6 for about 45 minutes, again until cooked through and the juices run clear.

Serve with sticky rice, *Som Tum Thai* (Green Papaya Salad, page 174), *Tum Tang Kwa* (Pounded Cucumber Salad, page 175) or *Soop Nor Mai* (Pickled Bamboo-shoot Salad, page 163), and with the *Nam Jim Jaew* (Roasted Chilli Dipping Sauce) of your choice (page 194).

Moo Yang Pee Kay

My Grilled Pork

I've had so many versions of this over the years that it's hard to pick a favourite or a definitive version. So this is my own take, based on a number of the Thai and Thai-Chinese barbecued pork recipes I've had. Serve with *Som Tum Thai* (Green Papaya Salad, page 174) or *Tum Tang Kwa* (Pounded Cucumber Salad, page 175) or, as they do in Loei and Nong Khai on the Laotian border, in a baguette with lettuce, pickled carrots and daikon (mooli), and some spicy Sriracha sauce.

Serves 4–6

4 small pork steaks or chops
2 tbsp thick soy sauce or *kecap manis*
2 tbsp light soy sauce
2 tbsp caster (superfine) sugar
4–6 garlic cloves, finely chopped
plenty of freshly ground white pepper
2 tsp vegetable oil

Make diagonal slashes in the pork chops without cutting through them and put them into a wide shallow dish.

Mix together the two types of soy sauce, sugar, garlic, pepper and the oil. Pour the marinade over the chops, rubbing it in and turning the chops in it. Cover and leave for a minimum of 2 hours, preferably overnight.

Heat a grill (broiler) pan until hot and grill (broil) the pork, basting frequently with the marinade, until cooked, dark brown and sticky, about 8–12 minutes.

Moo Khum Lanna

Lanna-style Grilled Pork

I've always believed that 'follow your nose' is sound advice for the food writer. And this recipe is a case in point.

I had taken some visitors to the beautiful Khum Lanna cookery school in northern Thailand and, while they were having their class, I smelt something rather delicious. It turned out that, just around the corner, they were cooking the staff lunch... this dish, sticky rice and *Som Tum Thai* (Green Papaya Salad, page 174). So I introduced myself and – hey, presto – managed to get the recipe. It's very simple and incredibly moreish.

I also like to serve it sliced in crusty baguettes, like a Thai *banh mi*.

Serves 4–6

400 g/14 oz pork collar in a single
    2 cm/¾ inch thick piece

3 tbsp coconut milk

1 tbsp coriander seeds

1 stick lemongrass, bashed and
    finely chopped

4 garlic cloves, peeled and
    roughly chopped

2 tbsp light soy sauce

1½ tsp curry powder

1 tsp pork stock (bouillon) powder,
    dissolved in 2 tbsp warm water

1 tbsp palm sugar

1 tbsp vegetable oil

1 tbsp oyster sauce

Make diagonal slashes in the pork. Pour the coconut milk over it and leave to marinate for 15–30 minutes. This is to tenderize and fragrance the pork.

In a pestle and mortar, pound the coriander seeds, lemongrass and garlic into a rough paste. Mix in the soy sauce, curry powder, pork stock, palm sugar, vegetable oil and oyster sauce, and stir well to combine.

Heat a grill (broiler) pan or barbecue (outdoor grill, medium coals). Shake off any excess coconut milk and slap the pork on to the grill. Baste the uppermost side with the sauce.

Cook the pork for about 30–40 minutes, until cooked through, turning and basting with the sauce as you go, until it's rich and golden brown, with some nice charred edges. Make sure you brush the sauce into the cuts in the pork to maximize the flavour.

When it's cooked, take the pork off the grill and set aside to rest for about 15 minutes. Serve sliced, with *Nam Jim Jaew* (Roasted Chilli Dipping Sauce, page 194) on the side.

Pla Pao

Fish Grilled in Banana Leaf

I love this method of cooking fish: the banana leaf imparts a particular flavour while retaining all the fish's natural moisture.

Traditionally, this is cooked on cooling charcoal. I remember buying this several times from a stall in the railway market just outside Pranburi, on the east coast. The stall-holder would tuck the banana leaf parcels into the coals, and spread hot ash over the top to cook both sides of the fish at once.

This method, though, makes things a little easier, so you can cook the fish over medium coals on your barbecue or on a grill pan on your stove-top, or even in the oven. You will also need enough banana leaf to wrap the fish securely. If you can't find banana leaf, you can use aluminium foil instead, but bear in mind that it won't taste quite the same.

Serves 4–6 as part of a Thai meal

1 banana leaf, washed (optional)
1 large (or 2 small) sea bass (see tip)

for the rub

4 coriander (cilantro) roots
  (see page 203), roughly chopped
a small bunch of coriander (cilantro)
  leaves, roughly chopped
4 large garlic cloves, peeled and
  roughly chopped
1 tsp black peppercorns
a large pinch of sea salt

First, wash the banana leaf, and set aside. If using a barbecue (outdoor grill), prepare the coals. Clean the fish thoroughly and cut diagonal slashes into its sides.

In a pestle and mortar, pound together the rub ingredients into a paste. With your hands work the rub into the fish and its slashes, making sure you don't waste any. Tuck any left over into the fish's belly cavity.

Soften the banana leaf by heating it over a gas flame or run it under hot water. It will instantly turn a glossy dark green and become malleable. Wrap the fish in the softened banana leaf, securing it with cocktail sticks (toothpicks) or satay sticks, and set aside for at least 10 minutes. If using the water method, make sure you dry the leaf before wrapping the fish.

Cook on the barbecue, turning once, until it is done. Alternatively, you can cook it under the grill (broiler), on a grill pan, or

bake it in an oven preheated to 200°C fan/220°C/425°F/gas mark 7. If you're baking it, you don't need to worry about turning it. On the grill, you must turn it once, halfway through the cooking time.

Which brings us to the big question: how do you know when it's done? This depends on the size of your fish. A small, farmed bass will obviously take less time than a big, beautiful, wild bass. My rule is to allow 10 minutes per 2.5 cm/1 inch. Measure the fish at its thickest point as it lies on its side, and calculate from there.

Serve with *Nam Jim Nong Da* (Nong Da's Dipping Sauce, page 194), or *Nam Jim* Seafood (Thai Seafood Dipping Sauce, page 195).

~ I've used sea bass here, but you can substitute any firm-fleshed fish you like. I think mackerel or sea bream work particularly well. ~

Yang Talay

Grilled Seafood

No trip to the seaside is complete without a grilled seafood feast. Whole fish, prawns (shrimp), squid, shellfish, *goong mongorn* (which means 'dragon shrimp', but really denotes a massive crayfish); grilled over charcoal; served with *nam jim* seafood; eaten with gusto. There's nothing better, and it is justly popular.

Outside any number of markets along the Thai coast, you'll find the grill guys waiting for you. All you have to do is enter the market, buy the most spankingly fresh seafood of your choice, return to the grill guys and let them cook it. There's normally a queue of people in front of you, but that's no hardship. They'll tell you when it will be ready, so you can slip away for a cold beer while your food awaits its turn on the coals. Then you pick it up and take it home. What could be better?

Of course, outside Thailand, we don't have that luxury. But you can still eat this way at home. So, what follows are a few tips to make it possible.

1. If you can't find the freshest seafood for this, don't do it. Similarly, if you're not going to grill over charcoal, don't bother. The whole point of this is the smoky, charred, open barbecue experience. For me, this means it's a weekend or summer holiday thing.

2. *Nam Jim* Seafood (Thai Seafood Dipping Sauce, page 195) is obligatory. For other accompaniments, I will tend to veer towards either *Som Tum Thai* (Green Papaya Salad, page 174) and sticky rice, or *Pad Pak Boong Fai Daeng* (Stir-fried Morning Glory, page 113) and rice. They're simple and satisfying, and uncomplicated. I want to give the fish my full attention.

3. When grilling prawns (shrimp), we normally mean tiger prawns (jumbo shrimp) or the larger king tiger prawns. How long they take depends on their size. As a general rule, an average tiger prawn takes about 1–2 minutes each side, and I recommend putting 4–6 onto satay skewers to make

turning them easier. King tiger prawns can take as much as 5 minutes each side, but again, size is everything. A timer won't help you much here. Your eyes will. You will see them change from a raw grey to a cooked, appetizing pink. Note, too, that they will cook faster peeled than in their shells. I prefer the latter as it keeps the juices in. Don't worry if the shells char. It all adds to the flavour and their aroma. You can also split the big prawns in half, lengthways, which allows you to devein them. If you do this, cook them on the shell side only. Again, you will see when they're done, probably in about 3 minutes or so, depending on size.

4. Fish should be grilled whole, with a couple of slashes cut into the sides to let the char in. Some people leave the scales on to protect the flesh, others don't. I prefer not. Rub them with vegetable oil on both sides before they hit the heat. If you want to stuff the cavity with herbs before you cook them, by all means do. Lemongrass, galangal, kaffir

lime leaves, all work well.

5. How long you cook for depends on the fish. My rule is to allow 10 minutes per 2.5 cm/1 inch. Measure the fish at its thickest point as it lies on its side, and calculate from there. Turn it once, halfway through the cooking time, just as you would with the *Pla Pao* (Fish Grilled in Banana Leaf, page 145).

6. Prepare shellfish in the usual way, cleaning the beards from mussels, de-gritting clams, discarding any that won't close at this point. Grill them until their shells open. You will lose some of their juices, but they taste amazing. You can grill oysters, too.

7. Squid, as ever, are tricky on the grill. We want them cooked, but not overcooked. Where Europeans in the Med often grill them gutted but whole, the Thai solution is to open out the tube into one flat piece and to score it lightly on one side. This should allow it to grill fast and roll up on itself.

146

Kai Toon

Steamed Eggs

This is a lovely, savoury custard, with a silky texture, which goes very well with spicy dishes – something to give your tastebuds some respite as part of a larger meal.

The balance of flavours plays an important role, not just in an individual dish, but also in the meal as a whole. And, for me, *kai toon* delivers a welcome, soothing note to a Thai feast.

Serves 4–6

vegetable oil, for oiling

3 eggs, lightly beaten

225 ml/8 fl oz/1 cup cold chicken
  or vegetable stock

1 tbsp *nam pla* (fish sauce)

freshly ground white pepper, to taste

1 tbsp deep-fried garlic (page 204)

2 spring onions (scallions),
  finely chopped

Oil a medium heatproof bowl with a little vegetable oil.

In a separate bowl, thoroughly beat the eggs into the stock to combine. Add the *nam pla* and the white pepper and beat again.

Put the garlic and the spring onions into the bottom of the oiled bowl. Pour over the egg mixture and steam, covered, for 15–20 minutes until just firm and wobbly. Serve with rice as a part of a larger meal.

Hoi Mangpu Op

Steamed Mussels with Lemongrass, Lime Leaves and Basil

Clean, healthy, economic and delicious – think of this as a Thai *moules marinières*. It's my perfect solo sofa supper in front of TV.

Serves 1, or 4 as part of a larger Thai meal

1 kg/2 lb 4 oz fresh mussels
1 tbsp oil
4 Thai shallots or 2 regular shallots, peeled and finely chopped
6 garlic cloves, peeled and chopped
1 large red chilli, sliced
2 sticks lemongrass, finely sliced
200 ml/7 fl oz/scant 1 cup water
1 tbsp *nam pla* (fish sauce)
6 kaffir lime leaves
a good handful of holy basil or Thai sweet basil, to garnish
wedges of lime, to serve

Clean the mussels thoroughly under running water, pulling off any beards they may have. If any mussels are open, give them a firm tap with the back of a knife. If they refuse to close, discard them immediately.

Heat the oil in a large deep saucepan (one with a tight-fitting lid) and sauté the shallots, garlic, chilli and lemongrass for 1 minute. Add the water, *nam pla* and lime leaves, and bring to the boil.

Add the mussels and bring back to the boil. Put the lid on and give the pot a good shake. Leave on the heat for 3–4 minutes, or until all the mussels are open and cooked (any mussels that remain closed are dead, and should be discarded).

Serve in a bowl, garnished with the basil leaves, surrounded by the delicious cooking liquor, and squeeze the lime over as desired.

Haw Mok Pla
Steamed Fish Curry

This was one of my Mum's favourite dishes, and one which she used to make frequently on Gozo. Although, as a concession to what was available there, she used to steam the curry in ramekins lined with cabbage leaves in place of banana leaves. When Dad gave me her recipe book after she died, I was thrilled to find her recipe, which I reproduce here.

Makes 8–10

1 banana leaf (optional)

150 g/5½ oz bamboo shoots, chopped

a handful of Thai basil

500 g/1 lb 2 oz white fish

2 tbsp red curry paste

6 tbsp ground peanuts (optional)

8 lime leaves, finely sliced

3 eggs

1–2 tbsp *nam pla* (fish sauce)

90 ml/3 fl oz/⅓ cup coconut cream, as cold as possible, plus 2 tbsp to garnish

1 large red chilli, finely sliced, to garnish

First, make the banana leaf cups: Soften the banana leaf by passing it over the gas hob (burner) or under very hot running water. You will see it change colour and become malleable as you go.

Cut out 2 banana leaf circles per cup, each with a diameter of 10–12½ cm/4–5 inches. Place the 2 circles on top of each other, dull sides facing inwards. Make a small tuck on the edge of each circle and staple it in place. Repeat 3 times at each point of each circle's compass, and voila! You have cups!

Alternatively, use ramekins – it's easier.

Place 1 heaped tablespoon of bamboo shoots in the bottom of each cup/ramekin, and a few basil leaves in each.

Dice about a third of the fish into small cubes and set aside. Put the remaining fish into a food processor with the curry paste, peanuts (if using), half of the lime leaves, the eggs, *nam pla* and coconut cream and blitz until you get a thick custard. Remove to a clean bowl and stir through the cubed fish and the remaining lime leaves.

Put the mixture in the cups/ramekins and steam for about 15–20 minutes until it has risen slightly and is cooked – test after 10 minutes. Remove from the steamer, garnish with a drizzle of coconut cream and the sliced chillies, and serve.

~ David Thompson gave me a great tip for this recipe when I moaned that I was finding condensation on all my custards. His hint was to remove the steamer lid slowly, and at an acute angle – stopping the water dripping from the underside of the lid on to the custards when going in for a test prod. Also, every time you remove the lid, wipe the underside thoroughly before replacing it. Cheers DT. ~

Pla Neung Manao Khun Mali

Khun Mali's Steamed Fish with a Spicy Lime Sauce

This recipe comes from my friend Khun Mali at the Puong Thong restaurant in Chiang Mai (for more about Mali, and how to find her restaurant, see page 164). There she makes it with snakehead fish in a massive Chinese steamer. I have replicated the process with sea bass, steaming it in the oven in a banana-leaf version of *en papillote*. I have also made it a meal for two using a couple of salmon fillets, weighing about 140 g/5 oz each (which will fit in my stove-top steamer), and dressing them with half the amount of sauce.

Serves 4

for the sauce

3 tbsp green Thai bird's eye chillies

3 tbsp garlic cloves, peeled

7 tbsp lime juice

7 tbsp *nam pla* (fish sauce)

2 tbsp caster (superfine) sugar

for the fish

1 x 1.4-kg/3 lb 2-oz whole sea bass, gutted through the gills (ask your fishmonger)

a good pinch of sea salt

1 stick lemongrass, bashed

1 coriander (cilantro) root (see page 203), bashed

1 banana leaf

First, make the sauce. Blitz the chillies and garlic together in a blender until smooth.

In a bowl, stir together the lime juice, *nam pla* and sugar, until the sugar has completely dissolved. Stir in the garlic and chilli mixture, and set aside.

Preheat the oven to 170°C fan/190°C/375°F/gas mark 5.

Season the cavity of the sea bass with salt and stuff with the lemongrass and coriander root. Wrap the fish first in the banana leaf, then loosely with aluminium foil, sealing it tightly while making sure that the fish has room to steam.

Bake in the hot oven for 25 minutes. Turn out on to a plate, peel back the skin and dress with the garlic-chilli sauce.

Pla Neung Kiem Buoy

Fish Steamed with Chinese Plums

With its soy sauce and pickled plums, its Chinese roots are obvious, and it's very popular in the south of Thailand, where you meet many Thai-Chinese descendants of the Chinese traders who settled there so long ago.

I have adapted this recipe from a version I ate at the Kan Eng restaurant on Hat Yai's Kimpradit Road. If you ever find yourself passing, please go and try and it for yourself – it's one of the best I've ever had.

Note that some versions require shiitake mushrooms and some minced (ground) pork or pork fat. I prefer to keep it simple.

Serves 4

1 whole fish, about 400 g/14 oz (I favour pomfret or butterfish, but tilapia and sea bass work very well)

3 pickled plums, plus 1 tbsp of their liquid

2 tbsp light soy sauce

2 tbsp oyster sauce

1½ tsp yellow bean sauce (optional)

1 tsp sesame oil

1 tsp caster (superfine) sugar

1 large red chilli, finely sliced

2.5-cm/1-inch piece of fresh ginger, peeled and finely sliced

a handful of Chinese celery leaves

1–2 spring onions (scallions), finely sliced diagonally

Wash and dry the fish, then cut a couple of slashes in each side, down to the bone. Set aside.

In a bowl, mix together the plums, their liquid, the soy sauce, oyster sauce, yellow bean sauce (if using), sesame oil, sugar and 2 tbsp water into a sauce, breaking down the plums a little with the back of your spoon as you go. Keep stirring until the sugar has dissolved.

Now, you can either put the fish on a plate that will fit into a steamer, or place it in a roasting tray, to be covered with aluminium foil. Pour the sauce over the fish, cover, then steam or bake in an oven preheated to 180°C fan/200°C/400°F/gas mark 6 for about 20 minutes, depending on the size of your fish.

About 5 minutes before the fish is cooked, uncover, add the chilli, ginger, celery leaves and spring onions (scallions). Cover again, and let it finish steaming.

Once it's cooked, remove the fish carefully to a serving platter, and pour over the juices.

~ If you're steaming your fish on a plate, the bottom of the fish may cook a little quicker than the top, so make sure you test it before serving. ~

Kraduk Moo Soi Thonglor

Soi Thonglor Pork Ribs

My Godmother, Shirley, lived for many years in an apartment block off Soi Thonglor in Bangkok. She was a terrific Thai cook and a barrel of laughs. She also had a budgie that perched on her head.

I remember this dish fondly as she would always make it for me on our monthly video nights (yes, dear reader, this was in the days before Netflix), accompanied by large and potent gins and tonic and a scary film.

It's the ginger-i-ness that makes this dish sing.

Serves 4

4 tbsp light soy sauce

1 tbsp caster (superfine) sugar

500 g/1 lb 2 oz pork spare ribs
(if you can get your butcher to chop them into 3 or 4 pieces each, all the better)

50 g/1¾ oz fresh ginger, peeled and slivered

5 garlic cloves, peeled and finely sliced

1½ tsp white peppercorns, roughly ground

In a small bowl, stir the soy sauce and sugar together until the sugar has dissolved.

Put the ribs into a roasting pan and pour the soy and sugar mixture over the top. Add the ginger and garlic, and the ground white pepper. Rub the marinade in with your hands until everything is covered, and leave to marinate for about 30 minutes.

Preheat the oven to 160°C fan/180°C/350°F/gas mark 4.

Cover the roasting pan with aluminium foil and bake the ribs for 45 minutes, then remove the foil, turn the ribs and put them back in the oven for another 30 minutes. Plate and serve.

Yums,
Laarps
and Tums

10.

Basic Yum

Beef or Seafood Salad

Yum literally translates as 'tossed' or 'mixed together'. By that virtue, you can make a *yum* out of almost anything, as long as it tastes titillating. These salads are not mellow, cooling dishes of leaves with a mild dressing. They cross the gamut of flavour.

Here is a recipe for a basic beef or seafood *yum*. The dressing can be customized to suit your palate.

Serves 4–6

2 tbsp lime juice

2 tbsp *nam pla* (fish sauce)

a pinch of caster (superfine) sugar

1 small red chilli, crushed or ½ tsp chilli powder

300–350 g/10½–12 oz rare grilled steak or grilled mixed seafood

2 Thai shallots or ½ onion, peeled and sliced

3–4 small tomatoes, quartered

½ handful Chinese celery or coriander (cilantro) leaves

lettuce leaves, to serve

Stir together the lime juice, *nam pla*, sugar and chilli or chilli powder in a large bowl, then toss together with the beef or seafood and the rest of the ingredients. Line a serving plate with lettuce leaves and pile the *yum* on top. Serve at room temperature.

Yum Mamuang Nai Muang

Green Mango Salad from Old Chiang Mai

I've adapted this recipe from a version made by a young woman I met in the weekend market in the heart of Chiang Mai's old town. It's simple, refreshing and delicious, and has become my go-to version. I love her addition of deep-fried crispy fish. Buy them dried and fry them off yourself, replace them with deep-fried dried baby squid or leave them out altogether.

This goes beautifully with *Peek Gai* (Chicken Wings, page 20), *Moo Yang Pee Kay* (My Grilled Pork, page 142) and *Moo Khum Lanna* (Lanna-style Grilled Pork, page 143).

Serves 4–6

1 tbsp *nam pla* (fish sauce)

2 tbsp lime juice

1 tsp palm sugar

1 tsp tamarind paste (purée, optional)

1 green mango, peeled and grated in strips

3–4 Thai shallots or 1–2 regular shallots, peeled and finely sliced

a good pinch of chilli powder

1 tbsp dried fried whitebait/anchovies/ Bombay duck or 4–6 dried baby squid (optional)

1 tbsp toasted cashew nuts or peanuts (optional)

coriander (cilantro) leaves, torn, to garnish

In a large bowl, mix together the *nam pla*, lime juice and palm sugar until combined and the sugar has dissolved. Stir in the tamarind, if using. Gently mix through the rest of the ingredients and serve straight away, garnished with the coriander.

Yum Hua Plee

Banana Blossom Salad

I think this dish is very special, not just because banana blossoms are in themselves so beautiful, but because it is one that redefines the notions of balance that people ascribe to Thai cooking.

The sweetness here comes not just from sugar but from the pork and the prawns. The sourness comes not just from the lime juice but from the subtle bitterness of the banana blossom. Its complexity delights.

You will find banana blossom at most good Asian supermarkets. Look for one that is nice and firm to the touch, and with as little discolouration as possible. If they don't look good, make something else!

Serves 4–6

1 banana blossom

1 tbsp lime juice, plus extra for acidulating soaking water

1 tbsp vegetable oil

100 g/3½ oz minced (ground) pork

100 g/3½ oz raw prawns (shrimp), peeled and finely chopped

1 tbsp coconut cream

4 tbsp coconut milk

1½ tsp palm sugar

1 tbsp *nam pla* (fish sauce)

1 tbsp *nam prik pao* (roasted chilli paste, see page 203)

2 Thai shallots or 1 regular shallot, peeled and finely sliced

1 stick lemongrass, finely sliced

1 mild red chilli, finely sliced

to garnish

1 tbsp unsalted cashew nuts, roasted

1 tbsp deep-fried shallots (see page 204)

a handful of fresh mint leaves

a handful of fresh coriander (cilantro) leaves

Take the coarse outer leaves off the banana blossom and save the best looking ones for presentation. Then, slice the rest of the blossom and soak it in acidulated water to stop it discolouring.

Meanwhile, heat the vegetable oil in a wok or frying pan (skillet) over a medium heat and sauté the pork and prawns until cooked, about 1–2 minutes. Remove from the heat and set aside.

In a non-reactive bowl, mix together the coconut cream and milk, palm sugar, *nam pla*, *nam prik pao* and lime juice to make a dressing. Add the cooked pork and prawns and mix them through the dressing gently. Then, add the shallots, lemongrass and red chilli, and mix gently.

Drain the sliced banana blossom, pat dry with paper towels, and stir through the rest of the mixture. Pile the mixture into the outer blossom leaves, scatter with the cashews, deep-fried shallots, mint and coriander, and serve.

Yum Haew

Water Chestnut Salad

At first glance, this recipe seems to involve a lot of prep and wok-ing, but it's actually very do-able and well worth the effort. It's a very old dish, and based on a version in Sibpan Sonakul's *Everyday Siamese Dishes*, the very first Thai cookery book written in English, and featuring food photography from the late King Rama IX of Thailand. I find its combination of flavours and textures very satisfying. It's also not spicy, just piquant, making it a useful *yum* to bring some balance to a meal.

Serves 4–6 as a part of a larger meal

1 tbsp *nam pla* (fish sauce)

½ tsp caster (superfine) sugar

1 tbsp lime juice

4 tbsp vegetable oil

2 tbsp finely chopped garlic (about 2–3 cloves)

2 tbsp finely chopped shallots (about 1–2 shallots)

2 tbsp minced (ground) pork

2 tbsp minced (ground) prawns (shrimp)

200 g/7 oz (drained weight) canned water chestnuts, drained, rinsed and finely sliced (see tip)

2 tbsp cooked crab meat

1 tbsp pickled garlic, finely chopped

2 large red chillies, deseeded and finely sliced

a handful of coriander (cilantro) leaves

Mix the *nam pla*, sugar and lime juice together. Set aside.

Heat 1 tbsp of the oil in a wok until it's almost smoking, and fry the garlic until it's golden, stirring it in the oil all the time to stop it burning. Remove and set aside to drain on paper towels. Wipe out the wok, add another tablespoon of oil, and repeat the process with the shallots, cooking them until they're brown and crispy. Set aside to drain.

Wipe out the wok again. Heat another tablespoon of oil and stir-fry the pork until it's cooked. Remove and set aside. Wipe out the wok, add the final tablespoon of oil, and repeat the process with the prawns.

In a large bowl, mix together the cooked pork and prawns with the water chestnuts, crab and pickled garlic. Add half the fried shallots, fried garlic and the sliced chillies, followed by the *nam pla* dressing and gently mix together.

Turn out on to a nice serving dish, sprinkle with the remainder of the fried shallots and garlic, some coriander leaves and the remaining sliced chillies.

~ *Quite often, you can only find cans of sliced water chestnuts. These work perfectly well for this salad. Just drain, rinse and pat them dry, and you're good to go.* ~

Yum Tua Plu

Winged Bean Salad

As much as I love this dish, it's not one I make very often because a) it requires quite a lot of effort, and b) it's hard to find good-quality winged beans. They just don't travel well. But, when you find them, it's really worth it. It is pretty spectacular. If you can't find them, but the mood to make this strikes you, you can always substitute them with runner (string) beans or, better still, asparagus.

Serves 4

100 g/3½ oz pork steak

vegetable oil, for basting and deep-frying

a pinch of salt

50 g/1¾ oz raw prawns (shrimp), peeled

1 tbsp dried prawns (shrimp)

2 tbsp unsalted peanuts, roasted

2 tbsp grated coconut, toasted

200 g/7 oz winged beans, trimmed
   and finely sliced

1 tbsp coconut cream

for the dressing

4 tbsp *nam prik pao* (roasted chilli paste,
   see page 203)

2 tsp palm sugar

2 tsp lime juice

2 tsp *nam pla* (fish sauce)

you will also need

3 wooden satay sticks or skewers,
   soaked in cold water

Heat a griddle (grill pan) until hot. Rub the pork steak on both sides with a little vegetable oil, season with salt and cook on both sides until it is cooked through. Set aside to rest.

Thread the prawns on to the soaked satay sticks/skewers, rub them with vegetable oil, and griddle (grill) them until they're just done. Set aside to cool.

In a small pan, heat a 2.5-cm/1-inch depth of oil until very hot, then deep-fry the dried prawns until golden brown. Set aside to drain on paper towels. When they are cold, grind them up in a pestle and mortar until they are almost completely powdered. Then add the peanuts and grind them coarsely.

Now make the dressing, whisking all its ingredients together in a small bowl until thick and well combined. Taste it for balance – it should be rich, salty, sour and sweet. Then stir in 1 tbsp of the toasted coconut.

Bring a large saucepan of water to the boil and blanch the sliced winged beans for about 30 seconds, then refresh them in iced water to stop them cooking. Drain, dry with paper towels and place them in a large mixing bowl.

Thinly slice the pork steak and add it to the winged beans. Cut the cooked prawns in half lengthways, and add them too. Finally, add the dried prawn and peanut mixture and the dressing, and bring the salad gently together with your hands.

Turn it out on to a serving plate, drizzle with the coconut cream, sprinking with the remaining toasted coconut, and serve.

Soop Nor Mai

Pickled Bamboo-shoot Salad

No, it's not a soup... it's actually a salad. This northeastern dish, fragrant with fresh herbs and toasted rice, has a very particular smell, which I immediately associate with Thailand, and which never fails to make me feel hungry.

If you possibly can, avoid the canned bamboo shoots for this dish. Instead, look for the ones in jars with *bai yanang* leaves, which I prefer, or ones which have been vacuum-packed.

Serves 4–6 as a part of a larger meal

2 tbsp *nam pla* (fish sauce)

2 tbsp lime juice (roughly ½ a lime)

4 tbsp stock (chicken or vegetable)

¼ tsp caster (superfine) sugar

1–1½ tsp chilli powder

½–1 tsp roasted chilli flakes

200 g/7 oz bamboo shoots, shredded

4 Thai shallots or 2 regular shallots, peeled and finely sliced

2–3 spring onions (scallions), chopped

2 tbsp ground, toasted rice, plus extra to serve

a small handful of coriander (cilantro), torn

a small handful of mint, torn, to garnish

In a saucepan, mix the *nam pla*, lime juice, stock, sugar and the two kinds of dried chillies over a low heat until the sugar has dissolved. Then, bring it to the boil.

Turn down the heat and add the bamboo shoots, shallots, spring onions, toasted rice and coriander. Stir together to heat through, then turn out into a bowl.

Allow the salad to cool slightly. Taste and adjust the seasoning if necessary – it should be hot, sour and salty. Serve, sprinkled with extra toasted rice and the torn mint.

Yum Kratiem

Garlic Salad

Mali Tiaree, who runs Puong Thong Restaurant in Chiang Mai with her daughter Anchalee, is one of my absolute Thai Food Heroes. She has spent many a painstaking hour (on her part) being patient with my *farang* ways. Gently chiding me, sometimes downright slapping my hand if my paste-pounding became slack, and generally giving generously of her time and knowledge.

If ever you're in Chiang Mai, please seek them out. The restaurant's right on the banks of the Mae Ping on the Chang Khlan Road, just around the corner from Rati Lanna Riverside Spa, which any *tuk-tuk* or taxi should know how to find.

Bear in mind that Mali cooks everything from scratch, so make sure you're not in a hurry. It's worth the wait.

Suffice to say, I'm thrilled that Mali gave me this recipe. I had never eaten this dish before I visited Puong Thong. I have never had it anywhere since. Thank God for it.

Serves 4

oil, for deep-frying

10–15 g/¼–½ oz cashew nuts (about 10)

2 large dried chillies

125 g/4½ oz raw prawns (shrimp), peeled with tails left on

75 g/2½ oz squid, cut into rings

2 Thai shallots or 1 regular shallot, peeled and finely sliced

4 garlic cloves, peeled and finely sliced

2 tbsp chopped fresh coriander (cilantro)

4 Thai bird's eye chillies,

juice of 1 lime

1 tbsp *nam pla* (fish sauce)

1 tsp caster (superfine) sugar

crisp lettuce leaves, to serve

In a wok, heat a 2.5-cm/1-inch depth of oil to about 170°C/340°F. Deep-fry the cashew nuts and chillies until the cashews are golden brown. Remove from the oil, and set aside to drain on paper towels.

Fry the prawns, until they have just turned pink and are cooked. Set aside to drain on paper towels.

Turn down the heat. You want to cook the squid '*chai wellah*', using time. It's a slow, almost desiccating process. Deep-fry the squid slowly, moving it around all the time, until it's crisp and dry and deep gold in colour. It takes longer than you think and, of course, depends on the size of your squid rings, so a minute-by-minute timing will not help you. Be guided by the colour and texture. Set aside to drain on paper towels.

Put the shallots, garlic and coriander into a mixing bowl. In a pestle and mortar, roughly pound the chillies. Add the lime juice, *nam pla* and sugar. Stir them together until the sugar dissolves. Pour over the shallot mixture and stir through. Snip the dried chillies into 2.5-cm/1-inch pieces. Add to the mixture along with the nuts and the seafood. Stir gently to combine and serve on a plate lined with lettuce leaves.

Laarp Isaan

Northeastern-style Laarp

Laarp can also be referred to as a salad by virtue of its being served frequently in lettuce leaves. This is a simple recipe for a basic *laarp* from northeastern Thailand, the region known as Isaan. It's the *laarp* most Westerners are familiar with – sharp, hot and salty, with the bite of chilli and fragrance of toasted rice.

Feel free to substitute the duck with pork, chicken or rabbit – just make sure you cook them through. Firm tofu can also be used, as can mushrooms for non-meat eaters.

Serves 4 as a part of a meal

225 g/8 oz lean duck, chopped or minced (ground)

1 tbsp *nam pla* (fish sauce)

1½ tbsp lime juice

½–1 tsp roasted ground chilli powder

4 Thai shallots or 2 regular shallots, finely sliced

1 stick of lemongrass, trimmed and finely sliced

1 tbsp toasted rice powder (see tip)

a handful of mint leaves, torn

lettuce leaves, to garnish

Bring a saucepan of water to the boil and add the meat. Bring the water back up to the boil, cooking the duck to your liking: it will take just 1 minute or so for it to be pink, a bit longer if you want it done through. When the duck's cooked, scoop it out into a bowl with a slotted spoon.

Add the remaining ingredients to the duck, and mix together well.

Turn out on to a plate lined with the lettuce leaves, and serve.

~ *To make the toasted rice powder, take a large handful of uncooked sticky rice (or normal Thai jasmine rice, if necessary). Place it in a dry wok or frying pan (skillet) over a low heat and toast it, moving it all the time, until it smells nutty and has turned a dark golden brown. Grind it up in a spice or coffee grinder, or in a pestle and mortar. Then keep in a jar and use as required.* ~

Laarp Kua

Northern-style *Laarp*

Traditionally, this is made with pork, pork offal and blood, which is earthy and delicious. Sometimes, decent pork liver is hard to come by, so I came up with this version, based around ingredients I could easily find. If you feel, after the first time you've made this, that you'd like it to be hotter, add more dried bird's eye chillies.

If you want to try it with pork and pork offal, use the same ratio as below.

Serves 4–6

for the *laarp kua* spice mix

1 tsp Sichuan peppercorns

1 tsp coriander seeds

4–6 dried Thai bird's eye (bird) chillies

1 tsp black peppercorns

3–4 green cardamom pods

2 star anise

½ cinnamon stick

1 whole nutmeg

2–3 cm/1 inch mace

3–4 Indian long peppercorns

1 tsp cloves

1 tsp salt

for the *laarp*

300 g/10½ oz minced (ground) duck

75–100 g/2½–3½ oz chicken or duck liver, trimmed and chopped

1 tbsp *laarp kua* spice mix (left)

2 tbsp vegetable oil

4–6 small garlic cloves, peeled, smashed or roughly chopped

1–2 tbsp *nam pla* (fish sauce)

4–6 kaffir lime leaves, finely shredded

2 spring onions (scallions), chopped

a handful of coriander (cilantro), torn

a handful of mint, torn

2–3 dried chillies, deep-fried, to serve

To make the *laarp kua* spice mix, toast all the dried spices in a dry pan until fragrant. Set aside to cool. Then, with a pestle and mortar or spice grinder, grind them together with the salt until they are as fine as possible. You should end up with about 4 tbsp of the mixture, which will keep in a clean jar for at least 1 month.

Mix the duck and the liver together with 1 tbsp of the *laarp kua* mix, and set aside to macerate.

Heat the oil in a wok until hot. Add the garlic and stir-fry until it's golden and crispy. Set aside on paper towels. Add the meat and the liver to the oil, and stir-fry until nearly done, about 2–3 minutes. Add the *nam pla*, and stir in the lime leaves, the spring onions and half of both the coriander and mint. Take off the heat, add half of the fried garlic and stir it through. Turn out on to a serving plate and top with the remaining herbs, garlic and the deep-fried chillies.

Serve with lettuce leaves, cabbage wedges or green beans and *kap moo* (Pork Scratchings, page 128).

Ruan Urai's Raw Tuna Laarp

Tucked down a small *soi*, or street, just off the mad bustle of Surawongse Road, in the midst of Bangkok's entertainment district, sits a haven of calm: Ruen Urai restaurant. It is set in a century-old teak house, tucked behind the mid-century Rose Hotel, and serves the most splendid Thai food. It's very much on my 'must eat here' list, if anyone asks.

The present owner, Dr Tom Vitayakul, was kind enough to give me the recipe for this *laarp*. I order it every time I go. Now, thanks to him, I can make it at home any time I like.

When I was testing it, I debated doubling the amount of tuna, but I've left it at just the 100 g/3½ oz here, because I think this dish is very rich, and it's enough. But if you want to make more, the recipe doubles easily.

Serves 2–4

1 tsp roasted dried chilli powder

1 tsp toasted rice powder (see tip on page 166)

1 tbsp fresh lime juice

1 tbsp *nam pla* (fish sauce)

1 tbsp finely sliced Thai shallot

1 tbsp finely sliced spring onion (scallion)

1½ tsp chopped fresh coriander (cilantro)

1½ tsp chopped fresh mint, plus extra leaves to garnish

100 g/3½ oz raw tuna, finely diced

2–3 small dried chillies, fried, to garnish

In a non-reactive bowl, mix together all the ingredients apart from the tuna until evenly combined. Then add the fish, and work it through the mixture. Turn out on to a serving plate, and garnish with fresh mint leaves and fried dried chillies.

Let's cut to the chase:
I could have called this
chapter 'salads'. And
all of them are, after a
fashion. But it's probably
best to paraphrase Bones
from Star Trek and say:
'They're salads, Jim, but
not as we know 'em.'

On Yums, Laarp and Tums

Of the three, *yums* are probably the most diverse. You can make a yum out of almost anything. Some are fiery, some are delicate; some are simple, some are complex. Of the ones in this book, which are among my favourites, I particularly point out the *Yum Kratiem* (Garlic Salad, page 164). Its name translates as a garlic salad; in fact it is a medley of seafood, garlic, cashews and spice in which squid is deep-fried at a low temperature for much longer than you'd expect until it's crisp and almost dried — a texture Thais adore.

Laarp can also be referred to as a salad by virtue of its being served frequently alongside lettuce leaves. I include three variants here, and there are many more, which can be found across the north and northeast. In Laos, they make one with raw buffalo meat seasoned with a little of its bile. Since those ingredients are hard to find, I have not included it here. But trust me when I tell you: it's delicious.

Som Tum Thai (Green Papaya Salad, page 174) is probably the most famous of all the *tums*, adored across Thailand and beyond. But it is by no means the only pounded salad. There are many, including one made with sliced raw green banana, which is… interesting. The Thais have a word, *faadt*, which describes that puckering, almost mouth-drying feeling you experience when drinking very tannic wine. This is the most *faadt* thing I've ever put in my mouth. So I've chosen to leave it out. But I have included other *tums* here, if only because the green papaya required to make *som tum* is an expensive ingredient, which is why you frequently find *som tums* cut with grated carrot. Not traditional, but a way to get by.

Som Tum Thai

Green Papaya Salad

Although a northeastern Thai dish, *som tum* is now ubiquitous across Thailand. Small wonder – it's fresh, feisty and delicious. There is also no definitive recipe. Each vendor brings their own touch and adapts it to each customer, often asking if you want it hot, spicy, sweet or sour. That said, this is adapted from a verbal recipe given to me by Khun Nok who works with her husband at their grilled chicken stall in Chiang Dao.

You will need a large pestle and mortar to make this. If it's made of wood, so much the better.

Photographed with sweetcorn on page 171, top right.

Serves 2–4

1 tbsp dried prawns (shrimp)

2 garlic cloves, peeled

2–6 Thai bird's eye chillies, roughly sliced (depends how hot you like it)

1 tbsp unsalted roasted peanuts, plus extra to garnish

a good handful of grated green papaya, about 120 g/4 oz

2–3 green beans, roughly sliced

1–2 medium tomatoes, quartered, or 4–5 whole cherry tomatoes

for the dressing

1 tbsp *nam pla* (fish sauce)

1 tbsp lime juice

1 tbsp palm sugar syrup (see tip) or 1 tsp caster (superfine) sugar

First, mix the dressing ingredients together, and taste for balance. If you want it sharper, add more lime; sweeter, more sugar; saltier, more *nam pla*. Set aside.

In a dry pan, fry the dried shrimp over moderate heat until they are just crisp. Set aside on paper towels.

In your pestle and mortar, pound the garlic and chillies just enough to break them up. Then add the peanuts and dried shrimp and pound until the nuts are loosely broken. Now add the papaya. Using the pestle and a spoon, pound and lift the papaya, mixing the other ingredients through it. Add the beans and tomatoes, and pound and mix until well incorporated. Add the dressing, and pound and mix again. The process should take no more than 5 minutes.

Turn the salad out on to a plate, garnish with the remaining peanuts, and serve.

~ To make palm sugar syrup, dissolve 4 tbsp of palm sugar in 4 tbsp of water over a low heat. Do not let it boil. Then set aside to cool. Strain it through muslin (cheesecloth) to remove impurities, and store it in a sterilized jar until you need it. ~

Som Tum Kowpot

Sweetcorn and Papaya Salad

You'll often find this variant made at the height of sweetcorn season. Grill a de-husked ear of sweetcorn on the barbecue (outdoor grill) or a griddle (grill) pan, turning often to make sure it cooks evenly, about 15 minutes. Cut the sweetcorn from the cob with a sharp knife. Then make the *som tum* as above, removing about 80 g/2¾ oz of the papaya from the recipe, and replacing it with the same amount of sweetcorn.

Tum Tua Yao

Pounded Long Bean Salad

Traditionally, this is made with long beans, which you can often find in Asian supermarkets. But green beans or runner (string) beans make a very good substitute, and most people would be hard-pressed to tell the difference.

The real key to this dish is not so much the beans as the *pla ra*, a thicker, more pungent variant of fish sauce from Isaan that is made of freshwater fish fermented with rice. My local Thai supermarket has a sign on its shelf saying 'this is not your regular fish sauce'. They're right: it's funkier, particular, and key to the broader range of Isaan's pounded salads.

Photographed with cucumber on page 171, bottom right.

Serves 2–4

4 Thai bird's eye chillies

1 garlic clove, peeled

1 tsp caster (superfine) or palm sugar

½ tsp *kapi* (shrimp paste)

300 g/10½ oz long beans, trimmed and cut into 5-cm/2-inch pieces

6 cherry tomatoes

juice of 1 lime

1½ tsp *nam pla* (fish sauce)

1 tbsp *pla ra* (Isaan fermented fish sauce)

In a large pestle and mortar, pound the chillies, garlic, sugar and *kapi* loosely. Add the beans and pound gently, turning with a spoon so they are all bruised slightly. Add the tomatoes and pound again, gently. Add the lime juice, *nam pla* and *pla ra*. Pound and stir to make sure everything is well amalgamated. Turn on to a plate and serve.

Tum Tang Kwa

Pounded Cucumber Salad

This was Mum's favourite thing to order when the *Tum* Man came down our *soi*. It is almost identical to the *tum tua yao*, above. To make it, replace the green beans with the same amount of cucumber, quartered lengthways, then cut into 0.75-cm/¼-inch slices. Give the cucumber a good pounding before adding the tomatoes which, in this case, I like to halve.

You may also like to add 2 tbsp dried prawns (*goong haeng*), pounding them into the salad at the same time as the chilli and garlic. In this case, pound the solid ingredients first, then add the *kapi* and palm sugar second. As an extra treat, you can also serve it with a peeled and quartered salted egg on the top. The combination of textures is very satisfying.

Tum Mamuang

Pounded Green Mango Salad

Again, this has almost exactly the same dressing. Simply replace the green beans with a good handful of grated green mango. Make the salad in exactly the same way. Serve with the *Moo Waan* (Sweet Pork, page 101), if you like. What a flavour bomb!

Desserts

Gluay Buat Chi

Coconut-poached Bananas

The direct translation of this dish is 'bananas ordained as nuns'. In reality, they're just bathed in warm, sweet and slightly salty coconut milk. Thai nuns' robes are white. So, too, are the bananas, hence their ordination.

This was a favourite of mine as a child, and I still make a big bowl of it whenever I miss home or feel a bit blue. You can rustle it up so quickly if you have all the bits in. If you can't find pandanus leaf, then either leave it out or use a drop of pandanus extract, which you can find at most Asian stores.

Serves 4–6

4–6 small bananas
200 ml/7 fl oz/scant 1 cup coconut milk
5-cm/2-inch piece of pandanus (screwpine) leaf (optional)
2 tbsp palm sugar or caster (superfine) sugar
a large pinch of salt
150 ml/5 fl oz/⅔ cup coconut cream

Peel the bananas and slice in half lengthways, then slice in half again.

Heat the coconut milk with the pandanus leaf and, when it comes to the boil, add the banana pieces, sugar and salt. Bring back to the boil and add the coconut cream.

Gently bring it back up to a simmer and let the banana cook for 3–4 minutes, until it is just giving but with a little texture.

Serve warm or at room temperature.

Som Loey Kaew

Oranges in a Sweet-salt Syrup

Incredibly refreshing in hot weather, and very simple to make. I love the salt-sweet-sour combo, but you could replace the salt with 1 teaspoon of rosewater, and even scatter a few rose petals over it before serving; or leave it out completely.

Serves 4–6

4–6 sharp oranges, peeled and pith removed, reserving one of the peels
250 g/9 oz/1¼ cups caster (superfine) sugar
½–1 tsp salt
crushed ice or ice cubes, to serve

Finely slice the reserved orange peel into thin julienne strips, and set aside. Then, segment the oranges with a sharp knife, cutting each one carefully out of its membrane. Place the segments in a bowl.

Put the sugar and orange peel strips into a saucepan with 450 ml/15 fl oz/scant 2 cups water and bring to the boil, stirring gently until the sugar has dissolved. Gently simmer until the mixture has thickened slightly, about 3 minutes in all. Remove from the heat and stir in the salt until it dissolves. Set aside to cool completely.

Pour the syrup over the orange segments, then chill until needed. Serve in individual coupes over crushed ice or ice cubes.

Sankaya Fukthong

Pumpkin Stuffed with Coconut Custard

This is a simple, yet stunning dessert. People will think you have spent hours on it... but you haven't. It's based on a recipe given to me by my friend Tuptim Malakul na Ayuthaya Lane. She in turn got it from the cook who worked for her family when Tuppy's dad was the Thai Ambassador to London in the 1950s.

It is one of those dishes that demonstrate the Portuguese influence on Thai cooking, though they would have originally made the custard with duck eggs. If you want to give it a go, just replace the 4 hen's eggs with 3 duck eggs.

Serves 4–6

1 small pumpkin or kombucha squash, about 20 cm/8 inches in diameter

150 ml/5 fl oz/⅔ cup coconut milk

85 g/3 oz/7 tbsp palm sugar or caster (superfine) sugar

a good pinch of salt

½ tsp vanilla extract or pandanus extract (optional)

4 eggs, lightly beaten

Slice the top off the pumpkin or squash, so that it forms a sort of lid. Scoop out all the seeds and any loose membrane. Wipe out with damp paper towels and set aside.

In a small saucepan, heat the coconut milk and sugar over a low heat until the sugar has melted. Stir in the salt and the vanilla or pandanus extract, if using. Remove from the heat and allow to cool for about 10 minutes. Pour the eggs into the coconut mixture and stir or beat well to make a custard.

Pour the custard into the hollowed-out pumpkin, then pop it into a steamer. Put the 'lid' next to it, so that steams too. Steam for about 45 minutes, or until an inserted knife or skewer comes out clean.

Set aside to cool, then chill until ready to serve.

Slice before serving – the whole slice is edible.

Tubtim Krop

'Crispy Rubies'

The word *tuptim* translates both as rubies and as pomegranates. You can probably guess why, but neither features here. Instead, water chestnuts are dyed red to resemble them. This is a very pretty dessert, and one that is relatively simple to make. (Behold the chemistry as the tapioca flour coats each 'ruby' with a glossy jelly!) However, if you have an issue with red food colouring, as some people do, you can leave it out. Though what you'd call this dish then, I've no idea!

Serves 4–6

1 x 400-g/14-oz can water chestnuts, drained and chopped
red food colouring (optional)
80 g/2¾ oz/generous ½ cup tapioca flour
120 g/4¼ oz/generous ½ cup sugar
200 ml/7 fl oz/scant 1 cup coconut milk
a small knotted pandanus (screwpine) leaf, or a drop of pandanus extract or jasmine extract (optional)
crushed ice, to serve

In a bowl, toss the chopped water chestnuts together with the red food colouring, if using, until they attain a bright ruby hue. Then, toss them with the tapioca flour until they are well coated. Toss them in a sieve (strainer) to get rid of any excess flour, making sure each piece is well coated, or you may get colour leaching later…

Bring about 500 ml/17 fl oz/generous 2 cups of water to the boil in a large saucepan. Add the water chestnuts and simmer for about 1–2 minutes – they are done when they rise to the surface. Drain and immediately refresh them in iced water. Allow them to get nice and cold otherwise they will start to stick together. Then, with your hands, remove from the water, separating any that may have become stuck together, and place on paper towels to dry thoroughly.

In a small saucepan, simmer 125 ml/4 fl oz/ ½ cup of water with the sugar until it has dissolved and is a little syrupy. Add the coconut milk and the pandanus or jasmine, if using. Heat, but don't allow to boil.

Remove from the heat and allow to cool completely. Place in the refrigerator to chill.

Place crushed ice in serving coupes. Divide the water chestnuts equally between them, and pour the coconut syrup evenly over the top to serve.

Ian Kittichai's Jasmine Flan

Ian Kittichai is one of my Thai Food Heroes, and quite simply one of the finest Thai chefs I know. He and his wife Sarah are among my dearest pals in Bangkok. He began cooking with his mother for the family's food cart every morning before school, and had no intention of cooking professionally until he came to London to study, working as a kitchen porter to make ends meet, and practising his English with the chefs in the kitchen. It was when he covered for a cook who hadn't turned up for a shift that his talent was spotted, and the hotel sponsored him through catering college. From there, he trained classically in Sydney before embarking on a trail-blazing career.

This simple recipe embodies his approach to Thai food, drawing inspiration from Thai cuisine and applying it to Western techniques. You can see this most clearly at his flagship Bangkok restaurant, Issaya Siamese Club. In this case, he takes the Royal Thai tradition of blooming jasmine blossom in water for cooking, and applies it to a classic Western dessert. Clever stuff.

Serves 4

1 g/heaped ½ tsp agar-agar powder or 3 g/1½ tsp agar-agar flakes

275 ml/9 fl oz/scant 1¼ cups double (heavy) cream

40 g/1½ oz/3 heaped tbsp caster (superfine) sugar

2–3 drops of jasmine essence

your choice of fruits for a fruit salad, to serve

In a small saucepan, bring the agar-agar and the cream to the boil over a medium heat. Add the sugar and stir until it has completely dissolved. Remove from the heat and stir in the jasmine essence. Divide equally between four ramekins and chill in the fridge for at least 2 hours, or until the flan has set.

Gently turn out on to chilled plates (see tip) and serve with a fresh fruit salad on the side.

~ Ian says that to make the unmoulding easier, quickly dip the ramekins into hot water and then shake it upright at a 45° angle so that the air gets to the edges and they pull away from the sides. ~

Condensed Milk Ice Cream with Buttered Croutons

This recipe comes from Jane Alty, who is the chef-proprietor of The Begging Bowl restaurant in south-east London. Jane comes from New Zealand; she fell in love with Thai food and cooking, and trained with David Thompson in both London and Bangkok, before opening her own place.

The genius thing about this recipe is... you don't need an ice-cream machine. It's perfection just popped into a Tupperware container in the freezer. The joy! Jane tells me this was by design. When she opened the restaurant, she had no space for any more equipment – and *voila!* – this was born.

As much as I love this ice cream on its own, it's my guilty pleasure to use it for a Thai-style *affogato*, pouring a shot of good espresso over the top of it. Here, I add a few crisp, buttered croutons to remind me of the toast and condensed milk breakfast I used to relish as a child. Thanks Jane!

Serves 6–8

7 egg yolks

50 g/1¾ oz/¼ cup caster (superfine) sugar

½ tsp sea salt

1 x 400-ml/14-fl oz can of condensed milk

½ pandanus (screwpine) leaf, knotted, or a drop of pandanus extract (optional)

500 ml/18 fl oz/generous 2 cups double (heavy) cream

for the buttered croutons

4–6 slices store-bought, thick-cut, sliced white bread

salted butter, for spreading

In a large bowl, beat the egg yolks with the sugar and salt until thick and pale yellow.

In a *bain marie* (a bowl set over a pan of gently simmering water, where the base of the bowl does not touch the water), heat the condensed milk with the pandanus leaf, if using, until it's very hot, but not boiling.

Remove the pandanus leaf from the milk, then pour the milk over the eggs, whisking constantly until fully incorporated. Return the mixture to the *bain marie*, and stir over the heat until it's thick and custard-y. Remove from the heat and transfer to the fridge to chill the mixture completely.

When chilled, in a separate bowl, whisk the cream until it has doubled in volume. Fold the cream and egg mixture together, making sure there are no lumps, and freeze in a covered container.

To make the buttered croutons, preheat the oven to 160°C fan/180°C/350°F/gas mark 4.

Butter both sides of the bread, trim the crusts and cut into cubes. Scatter over a baking sheet and pop into the hot oven. Bake for about 5–8 minutes. Turn, and cook for another 5 minutes, or until crisp. Keep your eye on them – they can burn suddenly.

Remove from the oven and set aside to drain and cool on paper towels.

Serve on top of the ice cream.

Mango, Lime and Basil Sorbet

This recipe happened by accident – the fickle finger of fate. I could not find a ripe, unstringy mango for love or money, but I wanted these flavours for a dessert. Then I remembered using cans when I lived in New York, because (again) I couldn't find fresh. They work a treat, and make this incredibly easy.

Serves 6–8

zest of 3 limes

100 ml/3½ fl oz/scant ½ cup fresh lime juice

a good handful of Thai basil

150 g/5½ oz/¾ cup caster (superfine) sugar

750 g/1 lb 10 oz (drained weight) canned mango in its juice (about 3 cans)

In a small saucepan, gently heat 150 ml/ 5 fl oz/⅔ cup water with the zest of 2 limes, the lime juice, basil and the sugar, until the sugar dissolves. Turn up the heat and simmer for 2 minutes to infuse the syrup. Remove from the heat and set aside to cool.

Strain the syrup, discarding the basil and zest, then add the remaining fresh lime zest. Pour the syrup into a food processor along with the mango, and blitz until smooth. Churn in an ice-cream machine according to the manufacturer's instructions. Turn the sorbet out into a lidded container and store in the freezer.

Remove the sorbet from the freezer about 5–10 minutes before you want to serve it.

I-Teem Kati

Salted Coconut Ice Cream

This is a very refreshing dessert that also happens to be vegan, something that has helped me out on many occasions when somebody's new boyfriend or girlfriend has arrived for dinner and only then dropped that particular bombshell. It's also simple and bloody delicious. Serve as is, or with mango to make a mango split.

For an extra blow out, pop a couple of scoops into a squishy white roll with a few peanuts, some corn kernels and gingko nuts scattered on top of the ice cream, and a drizzle of condensed milk – very Thai!

Serves 6–8

2 x 400-ml/14-fl oz cans of coconut milk
100 g/3½ oz/½ cup caster (superfine)
    sugar or palm sugar
a very good pinch of sea salt
150 ml/5 fl oz/⅔ cup coconut cream

In a saucepan, mix one can of coconut milk with the caster or palm sugar and the salt over a low heat, and stir gently until dissolved. Remove from the heat and stir in the remaining can of coconut milk and the coconut cream, making sure they are well combined – I use a small whisk sometimes, just because. Set aside to cool, then refrigerate until cold.

When cold, churn the mixture in an ice-cream machine according to the manufacturer's instructions. Freeze.

Remove the ice cream from the freezer about 10 minutes before you plan to serve it.

Nam Kang Gno

Rambutan and Rosewater Granita

2 x 565-g/1 lb 4-oz cans of rambutan in syrup
juice of 2 limes
2 tsp rosewater

Ice creams and sorbets are hugely popular in Thailand – and why not? They are the perfect antidote to the heat. This is an icy, sweet-sour crush, fragranced with subtle rosewater – perfect after a spicy meal.

Serves 4–6

Drain both cans of rambutan, reserving the syrup from one can.

Blitz the rambutans in a food processor with the reserved syrup, the lime juice and the rose water. Pour the prepared mixture into a fairly shallow glass or plastic container and place in the freezer, covered. Also pop a fork into the freezer to chill.

After about 1 hour, uncover and, with the now-chilled fork, scrape all the frozen outer ice crystal edges in towards the main body of the mixture. Re-cover and freeze again for another 30–40 minutes, then repeat the process. You may have to do this a few times. It should take about 3 hours. You want to end up with a beautiful pale, snow-like mass.

Keep covered in the freezer until ready to serve. You can make this up to a day before you want to use it, but no more than that.

Khao Neow Mamuang Lat Kati

Mangoes and Sticky Rice

250 g/9 oz sticky rice (cooked following the method on page 41)
250 ml/8½ fl oz/generous 1 cup coconut milk
60 g/2 oz/5 tbsp palm sugar or caster (superfine) sugar
a good pinch of salt
2-4 ripe mangoes, peeled, pitted and sliced
2-3 tbsp coconut cream, warmed, for drizzling
sesame seeds, toasted (optional)

When I started writing this book, every single one of my friends told me I had to include mango and sticky rice! People are obsessed with it. Please, please make sure you make it with decent, ripe mangoes, or it really isn't worth it.

Serves 4–6

While the sticky rice is still warm, in a separate pan, heat the coconut milk, sugar and salt until the sugar has dissolved. Pour the mixture over the warm sticky rice and stir to incorporate thoroughly. Cover and set aside for 5–10 minutes so that all the coconut can be absorbed.

Serve the still warm rice alongside the mango slices, topped with a little drizzle of warmed coconut cream and some toasted sesame seeds, if you like.

Dipping
Sauces and
Relishes

The Kruang Poong

Whenever you go for noodles or fried rice, you will find the *kruang poong* on the table in front of you (or someone will bring one to your table.) It is a quartet of condiments that allow you to season your meal to your liking. One pot contains caster (superfine) sugar; one *nam pla* or *nam pla prik* (fish sauces); one crushed dried roasted chillies; and one holds *prik nam som*, or vinegar with chillies.

Prik Nam Som
Vinegar with Chillies

Makes about 400 ml/14 fl oz

15–20 sliced long red chillies
6–8 garlic cloves
1½ tsp caster (superfine) sugar
½ tsp salt
425 ml/15 fl oz/generous 1¾ cups white vinegar

Lightly pound the chilles in a pestle and mortar along with the garlic.

In a small saucepan, dissolve the sugar and salt in the vinegar over a low heat, then pour the vinegar mixture over the chilli and garlic mixture and leave to steep.

Stored in a sterilized jar, this should keep for about a fortnight.

You could also just whoosh it all in a mini chopper or blender, once combined.

Vegan Fish Sauce

I have based this recipe on one I found on the brilliant *Vegan Miam* food and travel website and blog. It has proved a life-saver, especially when catering. For years, I was reluctant to offer Thai options for vegan clients, because although you can do a lot with soy sauce, I always felt I wasn't able to deliver food that tasted like I feel Thai food should taste.

This, however, gets as close as anything I've found to recreating properly the salty-funky quality that fish sauce provides.

Makes about 150 ml/5¼ fl oz

¾ tsp palm sugar
60 ml/2 fl oz/¼ cup warm water
60 ml/2 fl oz/¼ cup pineapple juice
60 ml/2 fl oz/¼ cup light soy sauce
salt, to taste

First, dissolve the palm sugar in the warm water. Add the pineapple and soy sauce, followed by the salt, to taste.

If the palm sugar hasn't dissolved completely, strain the sauce through a sieve (strainer).

Store in the fridge for up to 1 week.

Two Nam Pla Priks

Fish Sauce with Chillies

Nam Pla Prik or *Prik Nam Pla* (confusing, I know!) is the ubiquitous condiment, found on every Thai table. It's so simple to make and, boy, what a difference a drop makes!

I offer two versions here. The first is the classic, living up to its name: chillies in fish sauce. The second is a popular variation from southern Thailand.

Makes enough for one meal

Classic

6 tbsp *nam pla* (fish sauce)
10–12 Thai bird's eye chillies, finely sliced

Stir the chillies through the *nam pla* and serve. Apply liberally!

Southern-style

10–12 Thai bird's eye chillies, finely sliced
1–2 garlic cloves, peeled and finely sliced
¼–½ lime, finely sliced and cut into tiny segments
6 tbsp *nam pla* (fish sauce)

Stir the chillies, garlic and lime segments through the *nam pla* and serve.

Ajad

Quick Pickled Cucumber

This fresh pickle is served with so many things, from *Tod Mun Pla* (Fish Cakes, page 16) to *Gaeng Kari* (Yellow Curry, page 68). It's sharp, fresh and really easy to make. If you're making this to go with *Tod Mun Fukthong* (Pumpkin Fritters, page 18), leave out the cucumber, shallots and peanuts, and replace the red chillies with green ones.

Makes enough for one meal

100 ml/3½ fl oz/scant ½ cup vinegar
100 g/3½ oz/½ cup caster (superfine) sugar
a good pinch of salt
½ cucumber, quartered lengthways and finely sliced
2–3 Thai shallots or 1 regular shallot, peeled and finely sliced
1–2 mild red chillies, sliced
1 tbsp crushed unsalted peanuts (optional)
a small handful of coriander (cilantro) leaves, to garnish

Heat the vinegar and sugar in a small pan over a low heat with 2 tbsp water until the sugar has dissolved. Add the salt, then remove from the heat and set aside to cool.

Add the cucumber and shallots to the cooled mixture just before serving (it will go soggy otherwise), and then add the chillies and peanuts, if using. Garnish with coriander leaves.

~ This goes very well with satay and fish cakes, and they in turn are great for picnics. Just take the liquid and the chopped vegetables in separate containers and combine them at the last minute. ~

Nam Jim Jaew Song

Two Roasted Chilli Dipping Sauces

Classic

This goes with grilled or fried fish and meat, noodle soups, sticky rice – basically anything. The toasted rice gives it that lovely, nutty flavour.

Makes enough for one meal

3 tbsp *nam pla* (fish sauce)

3 tbsp lime juice

1–2 tbsp ground roasted chilli powder

1 tbsp finely chopped fresh coriander (cilantro)

2 small Thai shallots or 1 regular shallot, peeled and finely sliced

1 tsp toasted rice powder (see tip on page 166)

½ tsp roasted chilli flakes

½ tsp palm sugar

In a small bowl, stir the ingredients together. Set aside until needed.

With Tamarind

This version includes tamarind, which gives the sauce a rounder, sweet-sour flavour.

Makes enough for one meal

3 tbsp *nam pla* (fish sauce)

3 tbsp fresh lime juice

2 tbsp tamarind paste (purée)

1 Thai shallot or ½ regular shallot, peeled and finely sliced

1 tsp toasted rice powder (see tip on page 166)

½ tsp palm sugar

1 tsp chilli powder

1 tbsp chopped fresh coriander (cilantro)

In a small bowl, stir together the liquid ingredients, followed by the shallot, rice, palm sugar and chilli powder. Finally, stir in the fresh coriander and set aside until needed.

Nam Jim Nong Da

Nong Da's Dipping Sauce

My friend, Da, who lives in southern Thailand, made this *nam jim*, or dipping sauce, for us to take on an island picnic. It was the year after the tsunami had wreaked havoc on the area. But it had also brought with it the clearest ocean seen in years. We piled into Gop's boat and motored miles off the coast, to the Burmese banks. We rolled chickens in sea water and turmeric, built a fire to cook them, shucked oysters, drank beer, ate the chicken dipped in this sauce, and had a day so magical it couldn't possibly be replicated.

Try this with steamed or grilled fish or with the *Gai Yang* (Grilled Chicken, page 140), and definitely serve a batch with the *Yang Talay* (Grilled Seafood, page 146).

Trust me when I tell you, this is seriously HOT! The initial recipe has TWICE as many bird's eyes with just a dash more of everything else... Feel free to reduce (or increase, if you're feeling brave) the number of chillies.

Makes enough for one meal

5 garlic cloves, peeled and roughly chopped

15 Thai bird's eye chillies, roughly chopped

2 tbsp *nam pla* (fish sauce)

2 tbsp lime juice

1 large lime, sliced and cut into small triangles along the segments' lines

1 tbsp caster (superfine) sugar

a handful of fresh coriander (cilantro), chopped (optional)

In a pestle and mortar, gently pound the garlic and chillies until they're nearly a paste but still retain some texture. The more finely you pound the chilli, the hotter the sauce will be. Add the *nam pla*, lime juice and lime pieces, and stir together gently. Now add the sugar and a dash of water, if needed. Combine well, so that the sugar dissolves. Add the coriander, if using, and serve.

Nam Jim Seafood

Thai Seafood Dipping Sauce

This is the ubiquitous dip for seafood found across Thailand. Why it's called *nam jim* seafood as opposed to *nam jim talay*, I have no idea. But it is. It's a mystery...

Makes enough for one meal

6 green Thai bird's eye chillies, roughly chopped
2 garlic cloves, peeled
2–3 coriander (cilantro) roots (see page 203), roughly chopped
a pinch of salt
2–3 tbsp *nam pla* (fish sauce)
2–3 tbsp lime juice
1–2 tsp palm sugar or caster (superfine) sugar, to taste

Pound the chillies, garlic, coriander roots and salt to a paste. Add the *nam pla*, lime juice and sugar, and stir to combine. Taste and adjust to suit your palate – sharper, sweeter, saltier: these sauces are not an exact science, so shape it to your taste and around the quality and strength of your ingredients.

Add a splash of water to thin the sauce, if needed.

Serve with grilled (broiled), fried or steamed fish, prawns (shrimp) or squid.

Nam Jim Jao Fa

Peanut Brittle Dipping Sauce

Khun Jao Fa is another of my Thai Food Heroes. He's the executive assistant manager at the Tamarind Village Hotel in Chiang Mai, where – if you're fortunate – you can take his cooking class. This fabulous dipping sauce is his invention. I've cut back on the chilli and added some fresh coriander (cilantro) to soften and brighten it a little – but beware! It is still a spicy little dip.

Makes enough for one meal

3 coriander (cilantro) roots (see page 203), cut into chunks
3–4 garlic cloves, peeled
2–4 Thai bird's eye chillies (see tip)
85 g/3 oz peanut brittle, broken into pieces
2 tbsp *nam pla* (fish sauce)
2 tbsp fresh lime juice
1 tsp caster (superfine) sugar
2 tbsp warm water (you may need a little more)
1 tbsp chopped fresh coriander (cilantro)

In a pestle and mortar, bash and grind the coriander root, garlic and chilli into a smooth paste. Add the peanut brittle, and grind to a coarse texture, mixing it into the other ingredients as you go. Then add the *nam pla*, lime juice, sugar and water, and stir them into the sauce. Finally, stir in the chopped coriander. Turn the sauce out into a small bowl, and serve.

~ *If you would like to tone down the spice even further, deseed the chillies before you pound them into the paste.* ~

Nam Prik Num

Grilled Chilli and Aubergine Relish

Hailing from the north of Thailand, this is made with mild and fruity *num* or banana chillies, which can prove hard to find outside Thailand. I've found that the best substitutes are Hungarian wax chillies, Turkish Sivri, Anaheims or Poblanos. I sometimes add Thai bird's eyes, too. It's not traditional, but I like the kick, especially if I'm serving it with *Kap Moo* (Pork Scratchings, page 128) or *Moo Yang Pee Kay* (My Grilled Pork, page 142).

Serves 4–6

Photographed opposite, centre right

4 Thai round aubergines (eggplants), halved
3 large mild green chillies, halved
1 green Thai bird's eye chilli (optional)
6 garlic cloves, peeled
4 Thai shallots or 2 regular shallots, peeled and halved
2 coriander (cilantro) roots (see page 203)
a pinch of sea salt
a pinch of caster (superfine) sugar
1–2 tbsp *nam pla* (fish sauce)
juice of ½ lime
a good pinch of chopped fresh coriander (cilantro)

In individual aluminum-foil or banana-leaf parcels, roast the aubergines, chillies, garlic, shallots and coriander roots in a dry frying pan (skillet) until soft, about 15 minutes – turning from time to time. You want them to take on a grilled-like colouring, so open the parcels occasionally to see how they're doing. Alternatively, pop them all on soaked wooden skewers and cook over a griddle (grill) pan or barbecue (outdoor grill) until charred and soft.

Once cooked, let cool slightly. At this point, some people peel the large chillies and aubergine. I prefer not to – I like the flecks of char. Pound them together, with a good pinch of salt, in a pestle and mortar. You want a chunky, textured dip. Add the remaining ingredients and stir well. Taste for balance and serve with your choice of accompaniments.

Nam Prik Akha

Akha Hill Tribe Relish

The Akha are an indigenous people who crossed over into Thailand, Laos and Myanmar from China in the early twentieth century, with many settling in Chiang Rai, northern Thailand. It's a place I love, and I spend a lot of time far up in the mountains of the Golden Triangle amongst the coffee and tea plantations, scudding clouds and green, green forest.

This is a really simple, everyday relish. The Akha do not use fish sauce, so this is one of those things that happens to be both delicious and vegan.

Serves 4–6

Photographed opposite, centre left

8–12 cherry tomatoes
5 garlic cloves
4 red Thai bird's eye chillies
3 Thai shallots or 1½ regular shallots
1 stick lemongrass, finely chopped
½ tsp salt, plus more to taste
1 tsp yellow beans, drained or 1 sheet of fermented bean curd, toasted and crushed
juice of ½ lime, or more to taste
a handful of fresh coriander (cilantro), chopped
1 spring onion (scallion), trimmed and finely sliced

Char-grill the tomatoes, garlic, chillies and shallots until nicely blackened. Set them aside to cool. Once cool, peel them, but don't worry too much about getting all the charred skin off

In a pestle and mortar, pound the lemongrass and the salt together, or pop into a mini chopper. Add the tomatoes, chillies, garlic, shallots, yellow beans or bean curd sheet and the lime juice. Pound or blitz it together, then taste and add more salt or lime juice if needed. Stir through the coriander and the spring onions and serve with some raw vegetables and boiled eggs.

Nam Prik Kapi

Shrimp Paste Relish

Shrimp paste is a quintessentially Thai flavour. It lurks in greater or lesser proportions in all kinds of dishes, from curry pastes on. And it is a taste you either get or you don't. My friend Valerie loathes it. Fortunately, my husband loves it.

Serves 4–6

2 tbsp *kapi* (shrimp paste)

12 garlic cloves, peeled

9 Thai bird's eye chillies, plus extra to garnish

20 pea aubergines (pea eggplants)

5 tbsp lime juice

1 tbsp *nam pla* (fish sauce)

1½ tbsp dried prawns (shrimp), whizzed in a blender

1 tbsp palm sugar

a selection of vegetables, to serve: lightly steamed cabbage and/or pumpkin, winged beans, long beans, cucumber, boiled eggs and/or the *Cha Om* (Acacia Leaf Omelette, page 82)

First roast the *kapi* (shrimp paste): wrap it in some aluminium foil or softened banana leaf (see page 145) and heat it gently in a dry wok or frying pan (skillet) for 3–5 minutes. This really releases its flavour.

In a large, heavy pestle and mortar pound the garlic, shrimp paste and chillies together until you get a paste. Add half of the pea aubergines and crush gently. Then add the lime juice, *nam pla*, dried shrimp and palm sugar, and mix thoroughly. Add the rest of the pea aubergines and stir through. Then add a little warm water to bring it to the required texture – you want a soft dropping consistency.

Place in a small bowl and garnish with extra bird's eye chillies.

Nam Prik Ong

Northern-style Pork Dip

In general, *nam priks* are exceptionally spicy. This is the exception to the rule. It's sweet, fragrant and mild.

Serves 4–6

2 tbsp vegetable oil

2 Thai shallots or 1 regular shallot, peeled and finely chopped

3 garlic cloves, peeled and finely chopped

1½ heaped tsp good-quality red curry paste

125 g/4½ oz minced (ground) pork

2 tomatoes, finely chopped

2 tbsp *nam pla* (fish sauce)

1 tbsp lime juice

1 tsp caster (superfine) sugar

a selection of raw vegetables, to serve: cucumber, pumpkin, long beans, winged beans and blanched cabbage are all terrific

Heat the oil in a wok until it shimmers. Add the shallots, followed by the garlic, and fry, stirring all the time until golden brown. Stir the curry paste into the oil, cooking it out until it's fragrant. Then add the pork, and stir-fry until it's cooked through. Add the tomatoes and stir through. Then quickly add the *nam pla*, lime juice and sugar. Stir-fry for a couple more minutes. Serve in a small bowl, surrounded by the vegetables.

Nam Prik Kai Khem

Salted Egg Yolk Relish

Salted eggs are a great stand by to have in the
fridge – you can buy them hard-boiled and ready
to use in most Asian stores.

Serves 4–6

4 salted eggs
6 garlic cloves
½–1 tsp *kapi* (shrimp paste)
1 tbsp palm sugar
a good splash of *nam pla* (fish sauce)
1–2 tbsp lime juice
2 red bird's eye chillies

Peel the salted eggs and remove the whites from the yolks. Crumble
the yolks and set aside. Discard the rest.

Using a pestle and mortar, pound the chillies and the garlic to a paste.
Add the *kapi* and the palm sugar and stir into the chilli and garlic
mixture. Add the *nam pla* and the lime juice and stir them in, too.
Finally, add the crumbled egg yolks and stir in so that the *nam prik*
is well mixed but still has texture. Taste and adjust the seasoning to
your liking.

Turn out and serve with Thai pork scratchings and blanched
vegetables.

Pairing Wine With Thai Food

Most people thinking about drinking with Thai food will immediately head beer-wards. Or soft drink-wards. Or for a long and icy whisky soda. And there is nothing wrong with that – I love a cold ale or a tart glass of lemonade with my meal. But I really love wine with Thai food. And red wine at that.

'Red wine?' you say. 'What *are* you talking about?' The conventional, lazy sommelier pairing wine with Thai would guide you towards a Gewürztraminer or a Riesling. They're not completely wrong.

No. Scratch that. They are very, very wrong. Unless you like that, in which case, okay. Knock yourself out.

The thing is that there's no tradition of wine drinking in Thailand, so there's no conventional thinking on food pairings. Which means you can do what the hell you like.

My friend Kris Yenbamroong, who owns the Night+Market restaurants in Los Angeles, is a huge wine and Thai advocate. So much so, that he says he conceived the first Night+Market as a wine bar before anything else. His main pairing observation holds: with the robust flavours of Thai food, you don't want a drink that's overly complicated. To which I would add that you don't want one that's big on the tannins, either.

Of course, all wine opinion is profoundly subjective. But I urge you to try a few things to find out what you like. I lean towards the Austrian grape variety Grüner Veltliner for a solid white – it can stand up to a *gaeng som*, for which it has my utmost respect. Chenin Blanc always performs well. Soft, untannic Gamays and Cabernet Franc perform well with grilled (broiled) food.

But I do love my red, and I find juicy Argentine Malbecs particularly rewarding. My favourite reds with Thai are Shiraz or Shiraz/Viognier blends. They tend to be ripe, friendly, genuine wines. And if I had to pick just one, it would be a wine made by the legendary Bert Salomon in the Finniss River region of South Australia, a wine allegedly created to go with Thai food. Coincidentally, it just happens to be called Baan.

Kitchen Essentials

I have never been a fan of kitchen gadgets, mostly because I find most so-called labour-saving devices are anything but. That said, there are a few things you will need to make good Thai food. (I write this assuming you already have decent knives, chopping boards, saucepans… the general gear.)

You're going to need a wok, ideally two if you really get into this. (In the interests of full disclosure, I have seven.) A good wok is not expensive and it should not be fancy – the heavy cast-iron ones made by people like Le Creuset are not worth the time of day, though I almost always cook my rice in one of their lovely casseroles. Go to your local Asian supermarket and buy one there. Look at a few; put them on the floor to see which one's the most stable. Bear in mind that smaller ones are more suited for deep-frying than stir-frying.

Depending on the brand, you may have to scrub off a protective layer in hot soapy water; you may have to burn it off. The packaging will tell you. Then you have to season it: heat the wok until it's as hot as Gregory Peck, then add a couple of tablespoons of oil, moving it around the wok until the insides have turned completely black. Set aside to cool, then discard the oil, wipe it out with paper towels, and you're good to go.

From here on, your wok will generally need only to be rinsed and wiped out. When you do wash it up with soap, make sure you re-season it so that it doesn't rust.

That said, my most expensive piece of kit is a brass, two-handled wok that's 33 cm/13 inches across. I bought it in Thailand for deep-frying larger items, such as whole fish or *Sai Oua* (Spiced Northern Thai Sausage, page 28). It's brilliant because it conducts heat incredibly well and is extremely stable.

Most western kitchens lack a rice cooker. If cupboard space is at a premium, it's not a necessity; this despite the fact that the late, great film critic Roger Ebert once wrote a cookery book devoted to its use. But, if you're going to cook Thai food for a lot of people, for which read more than six, a rice cooker is a life saver. I find, however, that the 'keep warm' setting most of them switch into once the rice is cooked actually over-cooks the rice. So turn it off. The rice will hold its heat until you need it.

A pestle and mortar, however, is critical. By a pestle and mortar, I do not mean those little white ceramic things that look like a heavy teacup. Neither do I mean olive-wood ones from southern France, which have about as much purpose as a burst balloon. I am talking about a proper, stone pestle and mortar that looks as though it might give you a hernia the first time you lift it. And, if you really fall in love with the concept of *tums*, or pounded salads, a large one made of turned wood. With a good *tum*, we don't want to pound the ingredients to mush; we want to bruise them to bring out their flavour. Stone can prove a little much for them if you're not gentle.

Speaking of *tums*, one of the most useful things is a hand-held grater, which gives you the same effect as using the largest holes on a box grater without the attendant damage to your finger tips. Similarly, I cannot live without a good, fine-meshed deep-frying scoop. You should be able to find both in the equipment aisle of a good Asian supermarket.

Finally, I think a good three-layered steamer is really useful, and needn't be expensive. You can always use the bamboo types that go over water in your wok (although I've never really got on with them).

Glossary of Ingredients

Aubergines (Eggplants)

There are several types of aubergines used in Thai cooking, but of these, three are most commonly used. *Makeua yao* are long, skinny, purple or pale green aubergines, and are used grilled (broiled) in salads and in *nam priks* (relishes). *Makeua praw* are round, green, and about the size of a squash ball. They are used in curries, and are often served raw to dip into *nam priks*, too. *Makeua puang* are small and round and known as pea aubergines (pea eggplants). They're used in curries, stir-fries and dips. Unfortunately, when frozen they all tend to discolour to an unappealing shade of black, so it's best to buy them as needed.

Basil

The two most common Thai basil varieties are sweet basil (*bai horapha*), which is quite similar to European basil but with slightly more pronounced notes of cloves and aniseed, and holy basil (*bai krapow*). The latter has a skinnier, hairier, more pungent leaf and is the star ingredient in the popular *Pad Krapow* (Holy Basil Stir-fry, page 118). Neither freezes well. Lemon basil (*bai mangluk*) has a beautiful citrus aroma and adds fragrance to seafood curries and stir fries. If you cannot find the one you require, you can substitute sweet basil for holy basil, and vice versa. And if neither can be found, you can at a pinch make do with European basil. Just know that it won't taste quite the same — and change the name of the dish accordingly.

(Every *farang* Thai chef has now just thrown this book across the room in horror, because they don't realize that homesick Thais have been using European basil when they've had to for generations. You can put a bottle of fish sauce in your luggage when you travel; fresh *krapow*, not so much.)

Bamboo Shoots

These can be found in cans, in vacuum packs or slightly pickled in large jars with *bai yanang* leaves. In general, I favour the last of these because they keep well in the fridge. I always have a jar knocking around for an emergency *Soop Nor Mai* (Pickled Bamboo-shoot Salad, page 163). But if I'm making *Pad Normai* (Stir-fried Bamboo Shoots with Pork, page 121) I prefer the vacuum-sealed ones. The cans are there as a last resort.

Chillies

Where to start? You can buy chillies just about anywhere. But they are not always the *right* chillies. One leading supermarket sells packets of 'Thai chillies' that aren't Thai chillies. They tend to be cayennes — which will do at a pinch. But still…

There are several commonly used chilli varietals in Thai cooking, most notably the fiery tiny bird's eye (*prik khee noo*) and the mellower long-spur chilli (*prik chee fah*). Both can be found easily in Asian supermarkets. If you also find medium-long orange chillies while you're there, grab 'em. They're fabulous.

Fresh chillies freeze well, and you can use them pretty much straight from frozen. I tend to buy them when I see them, so my freezer always has plenty. They lose some integrity in form, but the flavour remains intact.

You will also need dried chillies — both long dried chillies and dried bird's eyes (which are known as bird chiles in the US) — if you plan to make your own curry pastes. You'll find the former in the Thai sections of most Asian supermarkets. I've generally found the latter there too, but some people tell me they've had difficulty tracking them down. In which case, dried African *peri peri* chillies are a good substitute. They are, after all, a bird's eye chilli too. They're just rocking under another name. Dried chillies keep for ages. I store mine in air-tight jars in the cupboard.

Coconut Milk and Coconut Cream

As mentioned before, most brands of canned or tetrapacked coconut milk are just not as good as the freshly squeezed stuff you can buy in Southeast Asia, or you can make yourself following the instructions on Page 63. In addition to the Aroy D Thai brand, I also recommend Clearspring Organic's coconut milk, and Trader Joe's if you're in the US. All three are broadly stablizer- and emulsifier-free.

If you need coconut cream specifically and, like me, think it's wasteful to open a 400-ml/14-oz can just for a couple of tablespoons of cream off the top of the milk, you can also buy smaller cans of about 160 ml/5½ fl oz. These, alas, contain additives, which inhibit the cracking process described in Page 62, but they'll do for garnishes or adding to a rich curry like Gaeng Panang. Most importantly, avoid at all costs the dried blocks of solid coconut 'stuff'. Or else God have mercy on your soul.

Coriander (Cilantro) Root, Leaves, Seeds and Stems
Thais use all parts of the coriander plant. Keep the seeds in the spice rack, the roots in the freezer (you'll generally find them in the freezer section of your Asian supermarket), and buy the leaves as you need them. They perish fast. Try to keep a fair bit of stem on the roots. If you cannot find coriander root – and there will be weeks on end when there doesn't seem to be any about – use the stems instead. It's not quite the same, but it'll do. If you become a super-keen Thai cook, buy it in bulk when you see it, and freeze it.

Dried Prawns (Shrimp)
In Thailand, you'll find these of differing sizes in markets all across the country, all for slightly different purposes. Elsewhere, you'll find them – usually the small ones – in packets either on the shelf or in the freezer section. They are used ground and pounded in certain dishes, or whole in *Som Tum Thai* (Green Papaya Salad, page 174). I keep mine in the fridge in a Tupperware container. Avoid ones that look too orange – they've been dyed.

Galangal
Ginger's cousin. It's easy to find in Asian supermarkets, so don't swap one for the other – ever – especially as it freezes well. Buy fresh if you can. The dried slices you find in some supermarkets are very disappointing, and the pastes are mixed with sunflower oil, which simply doesn't suit our purposes.

Kaffir Limes and Kaffir Lime Leaves
Some supermarkets now import kaffir lime leaves – and they're very good. The limes can be harder to find. Now they're generally coming in frozen. The leaves are too. They keep beautifully in the freezer.

Krachai (Chinese Keys or Fingerroot)
These roots have a hint of ginger about them, and are used to add fragrance and texture in stir-fries and curries.

Lemongrass
Another ingredient that freezes well, but is also readily available. When preparing it, it's best to remove the tough outer layers first.

Then give it a good bashing along its length with the back of your knife before you chop it. This helps to bring out the flavour, and makes it easier to break down if you're making a curry paste.

Nam Pla (Fish Sauce)
I always refer to Thai fish sauce as *nam pla* because its flavour is distinct from its Vietnamese relation *nuóc châm*, from the Italian *colatura*, and from the British Worcestershire Sauce, all of which are also 'fish sauce', leading to potential confusion and your food not tasting right.

To me, *nam pla* is the very taste of Thailand. It is in almost every Thai dish you will ever eat. If you're cooking for a strict vegetarian or a vegan, or someone with a seafood allergy, you should use soy sauce as a substitute (check the ingredients of any bought curry paste you might plan to use, too). You can also make the Vegan Fish Sauce on page 192, which approximates the funky flavour of the real thing. I favour Squid brand or the one from MegaChef. They're both made by the same people, so think of MegaChef as *haute couture* and Squid brand as *prêt à porter*. They are priced accordingly.

Nam Prik Pao (Roasted Chilli Paste)
This is not a curry paste or chilli jam – it's a whole different beast. Most people buy it at the Thai supermarket. The Mae Pranom brand is one of my favourites, but they're all pretty good.

Oyster Sauce
Most oyster sauces are not made with real oysters anymore. However, the MegaChef one is, and it is worth the extra cost. Other than that, they're all generally pretty serviceable. Mae Krua is my go-to for everyday use.

Palm Sugar
This is the primary sweetening element in most Thai food. Its quality varies. Sometimes you find it in grate-able hard blocks; sometimes you'll find it in a softer, more pliable form. It imparts a deeper, darker flavour than brown cane sugars. You can use cane sugar if you can't find it, but it's worth seeking out. While testing these recipes, I've confined myself to ones I can find in the UK, and the one from Thai Taste is pretty good. If you find that your palm sugar is too hard, and grating it to measure becomes difficult, just put it in a ramekin with a couple of teaspoons of water and microwave for 30 seconds.

Pickled Cabbage

You can use pickled cabbage or pickled mustard greens (*pak gard dong*) almost interchangeably, and you can buy both either vacuum-packed or in small cans. I use both, though I especially like to keep a few cans of the latter in the cupboard to serve with *Kow Soi* (Chiang Mai Curried Noodles, page 56).

Pickled Garlic

Kratiem dong in Thai and sold in jars in most Asian supermarkets, you'll generally be buying Chinese-grown European garlic, which has cloves about twice the size of Thai garlic. Not to worry – the flavour is basically the same.

Pla Ra

Fish sauce on steroids. Metaphorically speaking. This thick and pungent sauce from the northeast of Thailand is made by fermenting freshwater fish with rice. It's funky as hell, and I love it.

Preserved Radish

Hua chai po in Thai, this is also sold as 'pickled turnip'. It is the same thing: daikon (mooli). Generally speaking, it keeps for about 3 months once opened, and it freezes well if you want to keep it longer. I favour the Kirin Brand, if only because that's the one I see most often.

Rice

Rice is integral to Thai food (see page 39) and, even within Thailand, it comes in many forms. Most often, you'll want to use Thai jasmine rice, or sticky rice if you specifically want to cook Isaan or Lao food. Do not, please, use basmati rice. It's a lovely rice, but it does not go with Thai food. And to use American long-grain rice, also perfectly good in the right context, would be a crime.

Shrimp Paste

Kapi in Thai, this is one of Thailand's most prominent ingredients. When used front and centre as in *Nam Prik Kapi* (Shrimp Paste Relish, page 198), it's a wild taste sensation. It's used in most curry pastes, where it's often the ingredient that pulls all the rest together into a union of flavour. It's easy to find. Keep it sealed in the fridge.

Soy Sauce

There are three kinds of soy sauce: light soy, dark or thick soy, and sweet soy. They are not interchangeable. Buy small bottles of each, not because they go off quickly, but because of space. If you're using soy as a vegetarian substitute for *nam pla*, use the light version. There are several good gluten-free versions available if required.

Tamarind

Tamarind paste or purée is a big deal in the cooking of central Thailand. It keeps for ages in the fridge. I tend to use the Garden Queen Trademarked Concentrated Cooking Tamarind, which comes from Thailand and has a blue plastic lid. You'll find it in most Asian supermarkets.

Thai Shallots and Thai Garlic

These are both smaller than their European counterparts – by at least half – and they both tend to be slightly sweeter, too, but you can easily replace Thai shallot for regular shallot. Where you see '2 Thai shallots' in an ingredient list, assume one regular shallot will do as a substitution. As for the garlic, I have used European for all the recipes in this book – it just makes your life easier.

I place the two together here because you will often find one or both deep-fried as a topping or condiment. You can buy this in plastic jars at most Asian supermarkets, but it's very easy to make your own:

Very finely chop your shallot or garlic. Heat a 2.5-cm/1-inch depth of vegetable oil in a wok. When hot, add the shallot or garlic and cook, stirring constantly, until the shallots are nicely browned or the garlic is golden. Remove from the oil and drain on paper towels.

Turmeric

Fresh turmeric is *yin* and *yang*, pleasure and disaster. On the one hand, it imbues every dish with warmth, depth and colour. On the other, it stains your kitchen, utensils and hands to the point that it looks as though you smoke 120 a day. Wear surgical gloves. And use a dedicated chopping board. And realise that, when you're washing up, it will stain your scrubbing brush bristles a deep yellow. Consider yourself warned…

Yellow Bean Sauce

Confusingly, this can be labelled 'salted soybeans', 'soy bean paste' or 'brown bean sauce'. You can buy it as either a smooth product, or – my preference – with the whole beans in it.

Index

Acknowledgements

For as long as I have written about food, this has been the book I most wanted to do, so there are a lot of people to thank.

Firstly, Team Pavilion for saying 'yes'. Polly Powell – the powerhouse, Katie 'cool head' Cowan, Stephanie Milner – the Vidal Sassoon of editors: she makes all the best cuts, Helen Lewis – style and substance, Laura Russell – the cool factor, Komal Patel – press goddess! I've been to the Publisher Rodeo a few times now, so you know I know what I'm talking about when I say you're the best. Thank you.

Then there's Louise Hagger, ably assisted by Laura Heckford, for her beautiful photos; stylist Alexander Breeze for his superlative attention to detail; food stylist Emily Kydd, who didn't just cook everything, but also provided useful feedback on the recipes; copy-editor Emily Preece-Morrison for making sure of the prose; and to Bodil Jane (Folio Art), for designing the book cover of dreams.

There are literally hundreds of people across Thailand I should mention, but keeping my thanks specifically to this book, I am forever grateful to Somjai 'Mee' Kliangklom; Khun Tavee; Pee Noi; Khun Oot; Khun Pongsak 'Jao Fah' Siriphan; Khun Tieb Watjanakomkul and her sons Wattana 'Lek' Watjanakomkul and Warat 'Yai,' Watjanakomkul; Khun Thip, Khun Nai and all the staff – my 'pirates' – at Chao Lay restaurant, Hua Hin; Khun Tee; Mali and Anchalee Tiaree and their family at Puong Thong in Chiang Mai; David Thompson; everyone at The Fern in Mae Hong Son; Khun Jae Kee; Shirley Kinnaird; Tom Vitayakul of Ruen Urai; Khun Nok and Khun Tee in Chiang Dao; Tuptim Malakul na Ayuthaya Lane; Ian Kittichai and Sarah Chang – what they do at Issaya Siamese Club blows my mind every time; Jane Alty of The Begging Bowl; Nong Da; Loong Nern; and Kris Yenbamroong.

Diana Henry and Tom Parker-Bowles for being so encouraging and supportive; and Julia and Zack Leonard, Séan Donnellan, Debora Roberston, Fi Kirkpatrick and Melanie Jappy for eating a lot of Thai food and being the best chums.

My agent Charlie Brotherstone, for the faith (can I have those DVDs back, please?).

My butchers Grant, Jack, Linda and Matthew at Parson's Nose, Putney; and Mel, Simon, Khun Piak and Khun Mao Kriangsak at Talad Thai – people say I moved to Putney for their supermarket… all I can tell you is that the rumours are true.

My sister Kim, who remembers all of this, and the rest of my family.

And of course, my darling Fred – what would I do without you?

Oh… and Maya, Ruffy, Wilcox and Hepburn, the best writing companions ever.